Southern Living.

The
SOUTHERN
HERITAGE
COOKBOOK
LIBRARY

The SOUTHERN HERITAGE
Breakfast
and
Brunch
COOKBOOK

OXMOOR HOUSE
Birmingham, Alabama

Southern Living ®

The Southern Heritage Cookbook Library

Library of Congress Catalog Number: 84-062595
ISBN: 0-8487-0613-7

Manufactured in the United States of America

The Southern Heritage BREAKFAST AND BRUNCH Cookbook

Executive Editor: Ann H. Harvey
Southern Living® *Foods Editor*: Jean W. Liles
Production Editor: Joan E. Denman
Foods Editor: Katherine M. Eakin
Director, Test Kitchen: Laura N. Massey
Test Kitchen Home Economists: Kay E. Clarke, Rebecca J. Riddle,
    Elizabeth J. Taliaferro, Dee Waller, Elise Wright Walker
Production Manager: Jerry R. Higdon
Copy Editor: Melinda E. West
Editorial Assistants: Patty E. Howdon, Mary Ann Laurens,
    Karen P. Traccarella
Food Photographer: Jim Bathie
Food Stylist: Sara Jane Ball
Layout Designer: Christian von Rosenvinge
Mechanical Artist: Faith Nance
Research Editors: Evelyn deFrees, Alicia Hathaway

Special Consultants

Art Director: Irwin Glusker
Heritage Consultant: Meryle Evans
Foods Writer: Lillian B. Marshall
Food and Recipe Consultants: Marilyn Wyrick Ingram,
    Audrey P. Stehle

Cover: A serving platter of Scrambled Eggs and Rice (page 119) with
sausage links and bacon is surrounded by (clockwise from left) slices of
Pecan Loaf (page 25), orange juice, Orange Rolls (page 108), and
a bowl of grits garnished with bacon. Photograph by Jim Bathie.

Collection of Kit Barry, Brattleboro, Vermont

CONTENTS

INTRODUCTION

Coming out of Pennsylvania into Maryland, the traveler crosses Mason and Dixon's Line with no visible signal that he has arrived in the "South." For many, the first clue is the little side dish of grits that comes with his breakfast. It is discovery time; he may say, "What is it? I don't believe I ordered that." But, along with the grits, the hot biscuits quickly convince him that he has come to the right place.

Breakfast in the South is almost a cuisine in itself, if we may be forgiven a faint air of superiority. We base our claim on fact: Our breakfast and that later-in-the-day enlargement upon it we call brunch are founded upon the early Virginians' mastery of pork curing. With cured ham, bacon, and sausage as a point of departure, native corn was refined all the way from hominy and grits to spoonbread and batter cakes. Then came silky-fine flour, which, in the hands of Southern cooks, became the biscuit some people have lyricised as a sensuous experience.

Branching out from these three basics, we have in our repertoire unmatched meals with which to regale our families and to entertain some of our fanciest assemblies. Letters and diaries form the bulk of what we know of our forebears' breakfasts, and the critiques differ, depending on whether the writer was being entertained on a baronial plantation or taking his chances at an inn.

Breakfasts with George Washington are abundantly documented. In 1794, Englishman Henry Wansey wrote home that " . . . Mrs. Washington herself made tea and coffee for us. On the table were two small plates of sliced Tongue, dry toast, bread and butter, etc. but no broiled fish, as is the custom. . . . " Mrs. Washington served hot cocoa as well, and some guests enjoyed strawberry preserves for the first time at her table. The Eastern Shore fish-for-breakfast habit had made the scene by 1802 when Manasseh Cutler wrote of eating "red herring" at the Washingtons.

The agricultural South has always breakfasted early, usually by seven. Dinner, the main meal of the day, took place at two or three o'clock. This interval was improved in many homes with a second breakfast, more filling than the quick, early snack of bread, cold meat, and coffee or tea. In New Orleans, Mme. Bégué's Restaurant brought the "second breakfast" to a high art; we now refer to the meal as brunch.

ALONG THE WAY

For a rib-sticking and heart-warming breakfast, fill a platter with Fried Country Ham and Country Fried Eggs; surround it with Red-Eye Gravy, Grits, Old-Fashioned Buttermilk Biscuits, and Red Plum Jelly.

Williamsburg, Virginia, was already widely known for its well-provendered taverns in 1786 when a traveler wrote home from North Carolina that " . . . Travelers with any pretensions to respectability seldom stop at the wretched taverns; but custom sanctions their freely calling at the planter's residence, and he seems to consider himself the party obliged by this freedom." Civilization was still in the process of moving southward. The planter did welcome the wayfarer, regarding him as a link with the world. Good cooking meant home hospitality, not restaurant food.

Improvement in tavern fare paralleled the development of decent travel conditions. There were few notable roads before 1818, when the first section of the National Road was opened between Cumberland, Maryland, and Wheeling, West Virginia. Comfortable accommodations sprang up at coach stops, and plain but well-cooked food was available. General Andrew Jackson was one of the notables who appreciated the convenience of the crushed stone roadway. Breakfast was his favorite meal whatever the time of day; his invariable order at way stations was "ham and eggs."

Steamboats began to ply the Ohio and Mississippi rivers from Pennsylvania to New Orleans in 1811. As they rode the busy trade lane, the sternwheelers evolved into floating palaces for the well-heeled traveler; their dining rooms became legendary restaurants.

The first American locomotive in America, named "Best Friend of Charleston," was built by the West Point Foundry Company for the South Carolina Railroad Company and made its first trip in 1830. While this country's railroads, although well engineered, never reached the efficiency and serviceability of foreign rail service, they reached a zenith in luxury accommodations in the first half of the twentieth century. At first, restaurants of sorts served railway passengers at train stops, with the people being forced to bolt their food in order to get back to their seats before the journey continued. There followed dining cars with superb food, making rail travel the most desirable way of traversing the land.

Visitors coming south, by the turn of the century, found food that was second to none.

TAVERN BREAKFAST

olonial Williamsburg's taverns set themselves the goal of serving food their customers would have eaten at home—not an easy feat when guests were luminaries like George Washington and his fellow members of the House of Burgesses. Inns and "ordinaries" such as Christiana Campbell's and the King's Arms taverns still serve visitors fare similar to that enjoyed during the 1700s. Chowning's Tavern, patterned on the English pub, remains another haven of hospitality. The good tavern breakfast is a 150-year-old tradition at the Nu-Wray Inn at Burnsville, North Carolina, where Rush Wray carries on with hearty food in abundance served family-style.

FRIED COUNTRY HAM WITH RED-EYE GRAVY
GRITS
COUNTRY FRIED EGGS
OLD-FASHIONED BUTTERMILK BISCUITS
PEAR HONEY
or
SOURWOOD HONEY
RED PLUM JELLY

Serves 6

Richard Godwin

FRIED COUNTRY HAM WITH RED-EYE GRAVY

3 (¼-inch-thick) slices country ham (about 1 pound)
1 teaspoon bacon drippings
1 cup water

Slice ham in half crosswise. Set aside.

Heat bacon drippings in a cast-iron skillet over medium heat. Place half of ham slices in skillet, and cook over medium heat until browned, turning occasionally. Drain well on paper towels. Place ham slices on a large serving platter; keep warm. Repeat procedure with remaining ham.

Reserve pan drippings in skillet. Add water to drippings in skillet. Bring to a boil; remove from heat. Serve red-eye gravy with fried country ham. Yield: 6 servings.

A painting after a 1700s tavern sign invites travelers to take their ease with a favorite "dram."

Easy-to-make Pear Honey adds a sweet tang to any breakfast bread. Sourwood Honey (right) is a favorite.

COUNTRY FRIED EGGS

3 tablespoons vegetable oil
1 dozen eggs
¾ cup boiling water
Salt and pepper to taste

Heat oil in a heavy skillet until hot enough to sizzle a drop of water. Break each egg into a saucer. Carefully slip each egg into skillet, cooking 2 to 3 eggs at a time. Place one tablespoon boiling water on each egg. Reduce heat to low, and cover. Cook until whites are firm and yolks are soft or to desired degree of doneness. Transfer to a warm serving platter, and keep warm.

Repeat procedure with remaining eggs. Season eggs with salt and pepper, and serve immediately. Yield: 6 servings.

OLD-FASHIONED BUTTERMILK BISCUITS

½ teaspoon baking soda
¾ cup buttermilk
2 cups all-purpose flour
2½ teaspoons baking powder
½ teaspoon salt
⅓ cup shortening

Dissolve soda in buttermilk; stir well. Set aside.

Combine flour, baking powder, and salt in a large mixing bowl; cut in shortening with a pastry blender until mixture resembles coarse meal. Sprinkle buttermilk mixture evenly over flour mixture, stirring until dry ingredients are moistened.

Turn dough out onto a lightly floured surface, and knead 4 to 5 times.

Roll dough to ½-inch thickness; cut with a 2¼-inch biscuit cutter. Place biscuits on a greased baking sheet. Bake at 450° for 12 minutes or until lightly browned. Yield: 1 dozen.

PEAR HONEY

3 pounds pears, peeled, cored, and coarsely chopped
1 (8-ounce) can crushed pineapple, undrained
Rind and juice of 1 lemon
5 cups sugar
1 tablespoon powdered fruit pectin

Combine pears, pineapple, lemon rind and juice, and sugar in a large Dutch oven. Cook over low heat, stirring frequently, until mixture is clear and sugar begins to dissolve.

Stir in fruit pectin, and bring mixture to a rolling boil. Boil 30 minutes or until mixture registers 220° on candy thermometer, stirring frequently.

Quickly pour mixture into hot sterilized jars, leaving ¼-inch headspace; cover at once with metal lids, and screw bands tight. Yield: 3 pints.

RED PLUM JELLY

3½ pounds plums, washed and stems removed
2 cups sugar

Place plums in a heavy stockpot with water to cover. Cook until plums burst open and are tender. Remove plums, and place in a colander lined with several layers of damp cheesecloth. Gather edges of cloth up and over plums; squeeze to extract 3 cups plum juice. Discard seeds and pulp.

Return plum juice and 2 cups sugar to stockpot; bring mixture to a rolling boil, stirring frequently. Continue to boil until mixture registers 218° to 220° on candy thermometer or until jelly drops in sheets from a metal spoon. Skim off foam, and discard. Pour jelly into a hot sterilized jar, leaving ¼-inch headspace. Cover jar at once with a metal lid, and screw band tight. Yield: 1 pint.

BREAKFAST AT THE WILLIAMSBURG INN

Back in 1947, when Fred Crawford was Executive Chef at Williamsburg Inn, Duncan Hines stopped in to rate the food. In an uncharacteristic burst of enthusiasm he wrote Chef Crawford a note on the menu: "I could live on your delectable food! I would like to board with you, but I am beyond the age to take a chance on enjoying such rich food daily." Then, with a flourish, Mr. Hines bracketed the breakfast menu and labeled it "Perfect!" The thoroughly modern Williamsburg Inn is just outside the Historic Area, but it is nevertheless an important part of the total Williamsburg experience. Williamsburg cannot be "done" in a day; it is a common mistake for vacationers to exhaust themselves in the attempt. After breakfast, miles of walking, and lunch at one of the taverns, one needs to stay for one more "perfect" breakfast.

GRAPEFRUIT HALF WITH MARASCHINO CHERRY
PANNED SAUSAGE
BREAKFAST FRIED APPLES
EGGS COUNTRY-STYLE
VIRGINIA SPOONBREAD
SODA BISCUITS
STRAWBERRY PRESERVES
ORANGE MARMALADE

Serves 6

PANNED SAUSAGE

1 pound bulk pork sausage
3 tablespoons water

Shape sausage into 12 patties. Place patties in a large cool skillet; add water. Cover and cook over medium heat 5 minutes. Turn patties, and continue cooking, uncovered, until browned. Drain well on paper towels; serve immediately. Yield: 6 servings.

A sausage stuffer, known as The Genuine John Wagner Stuffer, c.1900.

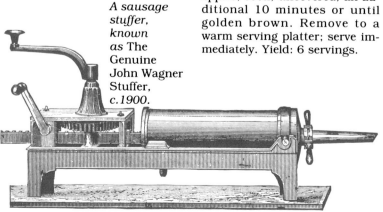

BREAKFAST FRIED APPLES

3 medium-size cooking apples, cored and sliced
¼ cup bacon drippings
3 tablespoons sugar
3 tablespoons firmly packed brown sugar

Place apple slices and bacon drippings in a large skillet; cover and cook over medium heat 10 minutes or until apples are tender. Sprinkle sugar over apples; cook, uncovered, an additional 10 minutes or until golden brown. Remove to a warm serving platter; serve immediately. Yield: 6 servings.

EGGS COUNTRY-STYLE

¼ cup butter or margarine
1 dozen eggs
Salt and pepper to taste

Melt butter in a large skillet, and heat until hot enough to sizzle a drop of water. Break each egg into a small saucer. Carefully slip each egg into skillet, cooking 2 to 3 eggs at a time. Reduce heat to low, and cook until whites are firm and yolks are soft or to desired degree of doneness, basting frequently with butter in skillet. Transfer to a warm serving platter.

Repeat procedure with remaining eggs, adding butter to skillet as needed. Sprinkle eggs with salt and pepper. Serve hot. Yield: 6 servings.

A Williamsburg breakfast at home: Eggs Country-Style with Panned Sausage, Breakfast Fried Apples, and Virginia Spoonbread.

Typical of the South's early inns was Fairview Inn, Baltimore, shown in T.C. Ruckle's watercolor, 1869.

VIRGINIA SPOONBREAD

1 cup cornmeal
2 cups milk, scalded
3 eggs, beaten
1 tablespoon butter or margarine
2 cups milk
1 teaspoon salt
2 teaspoons baking powder

Combine cornmeal and scalded milk in a large saucepan; mix well. Cook over medium heat, stirring constantly, until thickened. Remove from heat. Gradually add eggs and butter; stir until butter melts. Stir in remaining ingredients.

Pour mixture into a greased 2-quart casserole. Bake at 350° for 1 hour or until set. Serve immediately. Yield: 6 to 8 servings.

SODA BISCUITS

2 cups all-purpose flour
1 tablespoon baking powder
1 teaspoon baking soda
½ teaspoon salt
½ cup shortening
¾ cup plus 1 tablespoon buttermilk

Mix together flour, baking powder, soda, and salt in a medium mixing bowl. Cut shortening into flour mixture with a pastry blender until mixture resembles coarse meal. Add buttermilk, stirring until dry ingredients are moistened.

Turn dough out onto a lightly floured surface, and knead 4 to 5 times.

Roll dough to ½-inch thickness; cut with a 2¼-inch biscuit cutter. Place biscuits on a greased baking sheet. Bake at 450° for 10 minutes or until biscuits are lightly browned. Yield: about 1½ dozen.

Middle Plantation, later to be renamed Williamsburg in honor of King William III, was settled in 1632. Williamsburg was the capital of Virginia from 1699 to 1779. The town had only about 2,000 permanent residents, but during "Publick Times" the population could double. Spring and fall court meetings, the Assembly in session, or royal birthdays saw a bustling carnival of activity. Amiably situated between the James and York Rivers, the town, restored to its pre-revolutionary splendor, still hosts heads of state as well as millions of history-minded tourists every year.

PLANTATION VISITOR'S REPAST

English visitors to Southern plantations during the Colonial era wrote that breakfast back home was but a "meager repast" by comparison. Travelers of the day were almost all men, which may account for the frequent mention of the morning "dram," meat, and bread. But a few specifically referred to turkey, beef, venison, and other game. Margaret Hunter Hall, an Englishwoman who traveled from New York to the South in the 1820s, wrote a self-described "phillipic against the cooking in America" until she reached the Carolinas. From there she wrote: " . . . what shall I say of the breakfast! Such a breakfast! Such admirably boiled rice, such hashed turkey, broiled quails, and Indian corn flour which heretofore I have thought so bad, made into cakes of every description, each one more delicious than the other. . . ."

MINT JULEP
SLICED COUNTRY HAM
TURKEY HASH
CORNMEAL PATTY CAKES
FRIED GREEN TOMATOES
OLD-FASHIONED CORNBREAD
EASY YEAST BREAD
GEM MUFFINS
FIG PRESERVES
BREAKFAST COCOA

Serves 8

MINT JULEP

6 fresh mint leaves
¼ cup water
2 teaspoons sugar
Finely crushed ice
2 tablespoons bourbon
1 fresh mint sprig

Rub the inside of a chilled julep cup with one mint leaf, using the back of a spoon to gently bruise the leaf.

Combine remaining mint leaves, water, and sugar in a small bowl; mull gently until sugar dissolves. Add crushed ice, filling cup three-fourths full; strain water mixture over ice. Add additional ice to fill cup; add bourbon, and stir gently.

Chill at least 15 minutes. Before serving, garnish with fresh mint. Yield: 1 serving.

Official day starter for the planter and his guests was a cooling Mint Julep.

TURKEY HASH

2 tablespoons butter or
  margarine
¼ cup all-purpose flour
2 cups turkey or chicken
  broth
¾ teaspoon salt
¼ teaspoon paprika
⅛ teaspoon pepper
¼ cup sliced fresh
  mushrooms
1½ teaspoons butter or
  margarine
2 cups diced cooked turkey
2 tablespoons chopped
  pimiento
2 teaspoons chopped fresh
  parsley
Cornmeal Patty Cakes or hot
  cooked rice
Fresh parsley sprigs

Melt 2 tablespoons butter in a
large heavy saucepan over low
heat; add flour, stirring until
smooth. Cook 1 minute, stirring constantly. Gradually add
broth; cook over medium heat,
stirring constantly, until mixture is thickened and bubbly.
Stir in seasonings. Set aside.

Sauté mushrooms in 1½ teaspoons butter in a small skillet;
stir into white sauce. Stir in turkey, pimiento, and chopped
parsley, mixing well. Spoon
hash over Cornmeal Patty Cakes
or hot cooked rice. Garnish with
fresh parsley sprigs, and serve
immediately. Yield: 8 servings.

CORNMEAL
PATTY CAKES

2 cups cornmeal
2 cups milk
2 eggs, lightly beaten
½ teaspoon salt

Combine cornmeal and milk
in a large mixing bowl; stir well.
Let stand 5 minutes. Stir in
eggs and salt.

Drop mixture by heaping tablespoonfuls onto a hot, lightly
greased griddle. Turn patty
cakes when tops are covered
with bubbles and edges are
browned. Serve hot. Yield:
about 2 dozen.

FRIED GREEN
TOMATOES

½ cup cornmeal
¼ cup all-purpose flour
1 teaspoon sugar
1 teaspoon salt
¼ teaspoon pepper
4 medium-size green
  tomatoes, cut into ½-inch
  slices
Vegetable oil

Combine cornmeal, flour,
sugar, salt, and pepper in a medium mixing bowl; stir well.
Dredge tomato slices in cornmeal mixture.

Fry tomato slices, a few at a
time, in ¼ inch hot oil in a large
skillet until browned, turning
once. Drain on paper towels. Arrange on a serving platter; serve
immediately. Yield: 8 servings.

OLD-FASHIONED
CORNBREAD

½ teaspoon baking soda
1½ cups buttermilk
2 cups cornmeal
3 tablespoons bacon
  drippings, melted and
  divided
1 egg, beaten
1 teaspoon salt

Dissolve soda in buttermilk,
stirring well.

Place 2 cups cornmeal in a
medium mixing bowl. Add buttermilk mixture, 2 tablespoons
bacon drippings, beaten egg,
and salt, mixing well.

Place remaining bacon drippings in an 8-inch cast-iron
skillet; heat in a 425° oven 2
minutes or until very hot. Pour
batter into hot skillet. Bake at
425° for 30 minutes or until
golden brown. Cut into wedges,
and serve hot. Yield: 8 servings.

BREAD RAISER

EASY YEAST BREAD

2 packages dry yeast
¼ cup sugar, divided
¼ cup warm water (105° to
  115°)
2 cups milk, scalded
½ cup butter or margarine
1 teaspoon salt
2 eggs, beaten
6 cups all-purpose flour
2 tablespoons butter or
  margarine, melted

Combine yeast, 1 teaspoon
sugar, and warm water in a
large mixing bowl, stirring well.
Let stand 5 minutes or until
bubbly.

Combine milk, ½ cup butter,
salt, and remaining sugar; stir
until butter melts and mixture
cools. Add cooled mixture and
eggs to yeast mixture; stir well.

Gradually add flour, stirring
to form a soft dough. Cover and
let rise in a warm place (85°),
free from drafts, 1 hour or until
doubled in bulk. Stir dough
down, and turn out onto a heavily floured surface. Knead 1 to 2
minutes.

Divide dough in half, shaping
each into a loaf. Place in 2
greased 9- x 5- x 3-inch loafpans. Brush tops with melted
butter. Cover and repeat rising
procedure 30 minutes or until
doubled in bulk.

Bake at 325° for 35 minutes
or until loaves sound hollow
when tapped. Remove bread
from pans immediately; cool on
wire racks. Slice and serve.
Yield: 2 loaves.

*A loaf of Easy Yeast Bread
is flanked by Gem Muffins,
Cornmeal Patty Cakes, and
Old-Fashioned Cornbread
from "Indian corn flour."*

GEM MUFFINS

3 cups all-purpose flour
½ cup sugar
2 tablespoons baking powder
¼ teaspoon salt
2 eggs, beaten
1½ cups milk
¼ cup vegetable oil

Combine flour, sugar, baking powder, and salt in a medium mixing bowl, stirring well. Add eggs, milk, and vegetable oil, stirring just until dry ingredients are moistened.

Spoon batter into greased miniature muffin pans, filling three-fourths full. Bake at 400° for 15 minutes or until golden brown. Remove from pans, and serve hot. Yield: about 5 dozen.

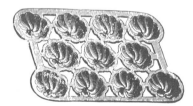

FIG PRESERVES

1½ pounds figs, peeled
3 cups sugar
1 lemon, thinly sliced

Combine figs and 3 cups sugar in a small Dutch oven, stirring mixture well. Cover and let mixture stand overnight at room temperature.

Cook fig-sugar mixture over medium heat until sugar dissolves, stirring constantly. Bring to a boil, and cook 10 minutes, stirring occasionally. Add lemon slices; cook an additional 10 minutes or until figs are tender and clear.

Carefully remove figs from syrup with a slotted spoon, and set aside; boil syrup an additional 10 minutes or until desired thickness. Return figs to syrup; skim off foam with a metal spoon.

Quickly ladle preserves into hot sterilized jars, leaving ¼-inch headspace; cover at once with metal lids, and screw bands tight. Yield: 2 pints.

The Olivier Plantation was painted by Adrien Persac, 1861. In 1862, the Louisiana sugar plantation burned.

BREAKFAST COCOA

1 cup sugar
½ cup cocoa
Pinch of salt
2 cups boiling water
1½ quarts milk, scalded

Combine sugar, cocoa, and salt in a medium saucepan; stir well. Gradually add water, stirring constantly. Bring to a boil; boil 3 minutes. Remove from heat. Stir in hot milk; beat 2 minutes with a wire whisk. Serve hot. Yield: 8 cups.

RIVERBOAT EYE-OPENER

In the early 1900s, the great stern wheelers plying the Mississippi began to evolve into floating palaces. Velvet and crystal decorated the ballrooms; linen, fine silver, and fresh flowers adorned the dining rooms. But it was largely the exquisite food and attentive service that secured the loyalty of the traveler. Even third-class passengers chose from a goodly list of breakfast dishes. Steamers such as the *Delta Queen*, the *Mississippi Queen*, and the *General John Newton* had almost limitless breakfast menus of fruits, hot cereals, meats, eggs, and breads. The Cincinnati-based *Delta Queen* still maintains a regular schedule to and from New Orleans.

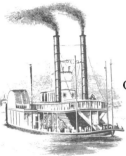

TOMATO JUICE ✳ HOT OATMEAL
BAKED APPLES
RUMBLED EGGS
SAUTÉED CALVES' LIVER WITH BACON
ORANGE PECAN WAFFLES WITH ORANGE BUTTER
RIVERBOAT HASH BROWNS

Serves 6

Group portrait taken just before a meal aboard a Louisiana riverboat, c.1900.

Sautéed Calves' Liver with Bacon and butter-rich Rumbled Eggs make a hearty breakfast.

ORANGE PECAN WAFFLES WITH ORANGE BUTTER

1½ cups all-purpose flour
1 tablespoon plus 1 teaspoon baking powder
1 tablespoon sugar
½ teaspoon salt
1 cup milk
3 eggs, beaten
½ cup orange marmalade
¼ cup shortening, melted
½ cup finely chopped pecans, toasted
Orange Butter

Combine first 4 ingredients in a medium mixing bowl; stir well. Combine milk, eggs, marmalade, and shortening in a small mixing bowl; beat well. Add milk mixture to flour mixture, mixing until blended. Stir in pecans.

Spoon batter onto a preheated, lightly oiled waffle iron, following manufacturer's directions. Cook 5 minutes or until browned and crisp. Remove waffle, and keep warm. Repeat procedure with remaining batter. Serve waffles warm with Orange Butter. Yield: sixteen 4-inch waffles.

Orange Butter:

½ cup butter, softened
¼ cup orange marmalade

Cream butter in a small mixing bowl. Add marmalade; beat until well blended. Chill until ready to use. Yield: about ½ cup.

BAKED APPLES

6 large baking apples
1 lemon
1 cup hot water
2 tablespoons sugar
Whipping cream (optional)

Core apples; peel top third of each. Divide lemon into 6 wedges; stuff 1 wedge into cavity of each apple, and set aside.

Combine water and sugar in a shallow baking dish; stir well. Place apples in dish. Bake at 350° for 45 minutes or until tender, basting occasionally with pan liquid. Serve hot or cold with whipping cream, if desired. Yield: 6 servings.

RUMBLED EGGS

9 eggs, beaten
½ cup butter or margarine, melted
1 tablespoon whipping cream

Combine eggs and butter in a medium mixing bowl, stirring well. Add whipping cream; mix well. Pour egg mixture into a medium saucepan; cook over medium heat, stirring often, until eggs are firm but still moist. Spoon onto a warm serving platter, and serve immediately. Yield: 6 servings.

SAUTÉED CALVES' LIVER WITH BACON

1½ pounds thinly sliced calves' liver
Salt and pepper to taste
½ cup all-purpose flour
12 slices bacon
1 medium onion, thinly sliced
Fresh parsley sprigs

Sprinkle liver with salt and pepper; dredge in flour, and set aside.

Cook bacon in a heavy skillet until crisp; remove bacon, reserving 2 tablespoons pan drippings in skillet. Drain bacon on paper towels; set aside.

Cook liver in pan drippings over medium heat until browned on both sides; top with onion slices. Cover and simmer 20 minutes or until liver is no longer pink.

Transfer liver and onion slices to a warm serving platter; garnish with reserved bacon and parsley sprigs. Serve immediately. Yield: 6 servings.

The Great Mississippi Steamboat Race of 1870 made river history. Captain John Cannon of the *Natchez* and Captain Thomas P. Leathers of the *Robert E. Lee* were partners-turned-enemies. The race was a culmination of their animosity, and ended with the *Lee* setting a speed record for the New Orleans to St. Louis run.

The Celebrated Race of the Steamers Robt. E. Lee and Natchez, *a color lithograph, 1883.*

RIVERBOAT HASH BROWNS

4 large potatoes, boiled,
   peeled, and coarsely grated
   (about 4 cups)
1 small onion, finely chopped
1 teaspoon salt
1 teaspoon chili powder
¼ teaspoon pepper
3 tablespoons butter or
   margarine, divided
3 tablespoons bacon
   drippings, divided

Combine grated potatoes,

onion, salt, chili powder, and pepper in a large mixing bowl; toss lightly.

Heat 2 tablespoons butter and 2 tablespoons bacon drippings in a heavy 10-inch skillet over medium heat. Add potato mixture, spreading evenly over bottom of skillet using a spatula. Press potatoes down forming a flat cake. Use spatula to loosen edges from side of skillet, if necessary. Cook 10 minutes or

until bottom is browned and crusty.

Remove skillet from heat. Place a large plate over skillet; invert potato cake onto plate.

Melt remaining butter and bacon drippings in skillet over medium heat; slide potato cake back into skillet. Cook 10 minutes or until bottom is browned and crusty. Invert onto a serving plate. Cut into wedges, and serve. Yield: 8 servings.

BREAKFAST ON A TRAIN

Railways and their dining cars were enjoying their heyday when World War II erupted. Before 1942, the ultimate adventure for a Southerner was to board a Southern Railway Company train for an overnight journey to New York. Mealtime on the dining car: Rows of white-linened tables, each with a bud vase of fresh flowers on the window end, white-coated waiters holding trays over their heads, nimbly avoiding collisions in the aisles. Breakfast menus led off with steak and eggs and featured the best coffee in the land. Sadly, today's train travel, if it works at all, does not resemble that of yesteryear. Here, then, is a nostalgic menu from another time.

STEAK AND EGGS
LYONNAISE POTATOES
BUCKWHEAT CAKES WITH SYRUP
APPLE PIE
or
BAKED BANANAS

Serves 8

STEAK AND EGGS

8 (½-inch-thick) club steaks
  (about 4 pounds)
1 teaspoon salt
½ teaspoon pepper
¼ cup bacon drippings
8 eggs
Spiced crabapples

Place 2 steaks in a large skillet. Brown quickly on both sides over medium-high heat; sprinkle steaks with salt and pepper. Reduce heat to low; cook until desired degree of doneness, turning occasionally. Remove steaks to a warm platter; keep warm. Repeat procedure with remaining steaks.

Heat bacon drippings in a large skillet over medium heat. Break each egg into a saucer. Carefully slip each egg into skillet, cooking 2 to 3 eggs at a time. Reduce heat to low. Cook 1 minute or until egg whites are set. Turn eggs; cook until desired degree of doneness. Carefully remove eggs, and place 1 egg on top of each steak. Repeat procedure with remaining eggs. Garnish platter with crabapples, and serve. Yield: 8 servings.

Mealtime on the train was an elegant affair with full course meals, c.1895.

Brown Brothers

LYONNAISE POTATOES

3 pounds new potatoes,
  peeled
Vegetable oil
2 large onions, sliced
Salt and pepper to taste

Place potatoes in a large Dutch oven with water to cover. Bring to a boil; cook 5 minutes. Drain well; slice potatoes into ³⁄₈-inch-thick slices.

Heat oil in a large skillet over medium-high heat. Arrange half of potato and onion slices in a single layer in skillet. Sprinkle with salt and pepper. Cook, turning frequently, until onions are tender and potatoes are golden brown; drain. Transfer potatoes and onions to a serving dish. Repeat procedure with remaining potato and onion slices. Yield: 8 servings.

Pictured in a restored dining car, Apple Pie for two.

BUCKWHEAT CAKES

1½ cups sifted buckwheat
  flour
½ cup all-purpose flour
1 teaspoon baking soda
1 teaspoon salt
3 cups buttermilk
1 tablespoon molasses
1 tablespoon vegetable oil
Butter or margarine, melted
Syrup

Sift together flour, soda, and salt into a mixing bowl. Combine buttermilk and molasses; stir well. Add buttermilk mixture to flour mixture, stirring just until smooth. Stir in oil.

For each pancake, pour ¼ cup batter onto a hot, well-greased griddle. Turn when tops are covered with bubbles and edges are slightly dry. Serve hot with butter and syrup. Yield: sixteen 4-inch pancakes.

APPLE PIE

2 cups all-purpose flour
½ teaspoon salt
¾ cup shortening
4 to 6 tablespoons cold water
6 medium-size cooking
  apples, peeled, cored, and
  quartered
¼ cup water, divided
½ cup sugar
1 teaspoon butter or
  margarine
¼ teaspoon ground cinnamon

Combine flour and salt in a medium mixing bowl; cut in shortening with a pastry blender until mixture resembles coarse meal. Sprinkle 4 to 6 tablespoons cold water over flour mixture; stir with a fork until dry ingredients are moistened. Shape dough into a ball; chill.

Roll half of pastry to ⅛-inch thickness on a lightly floured surface; fit pastry into a 9-inch pieplate. Place apple slices in pieplate; sprinkle with 2 tablespoons water.

Roll remaining pastry to ⅛-inch thickness, and place over apple slices. Trim edges; seal and flute. Cut several long slits in top crust. Bake at 375° for 55 minutes or until golden brown.

Remove from oven; set aside.

Combine 2 tablespoons water, sugar, butter, and cinnamon in a small saucepan; bring to a boil. Pour syrup into pie through slits in top crust. Cool pie before cutting. Yield: one 9-inch double-crust pie.

BAKED BANANAS

4 bananas, peeled
Lemon juice
¼ cup raisins
¼ cup finely chopped pecans
½ cup sugar
¼ cup light corn syrup
¼ cup water
1 tablespoon butter or
  margarine
Whipping cream (optional)

Dip bananas in lemon juice; arrange in a greased 2-quart baking dish. Sprinkle with raisins and pecans. Combine sugar, syrup, and water in a small saucepan; cook over medium heat until bubbly. Spoon syrup over bananas; dot with butter. Cover and bake at 350° for 25 minutes. Serve warm with whipping cream, if desired. Yield: 8 servings.

ROOM SERVICE

A young woman who came as a tutor to a Tennessee planter's child wrote of being served a wine mint julep and coffee while still in bed. It was 1853: ". . . I had been raised in the plain simple Yankee way. . . ." She banished the luxuries forthwith. Once commonplace on plantations in the Old South, breakfast in one's room is now mostly a memory. The magic is still there, in fine hotels and resorts: A rap on the door, a voice announcing, "Room service," and for a moment, we taste the easeful life. Sometimes a family member will do the honors at home; even if it's just a tray with juice and coffee and a single posey, nothing says "you're pampered" like room service!

WINE COOLER
FRESH FRUIT IN SEASON
or
STEWED MIXED FRUITS
BROILED CORNISH HENS
BAKED TOMATO HALVES
PECAN LOAF
COFFEE

Serves 4

"Man's best friend" may be allowed to share the bed, but not breakfast therein.

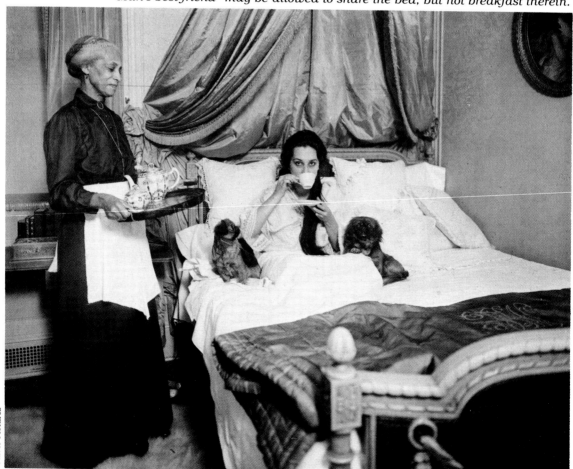

Wine Cooler and fresh fruit to start the day.

WINE COOLER

Shaved ice
2 cups Chablis or other dry white wine
2 cups lemon-lime carbonated beverage
Lemon twists

Fill 4 tall glasses with shaved ice. Pour ½ cup wine into each glass. Fill glass with lemon-lime beverage. Stir slightly. Garnish glasses with lemon twists. Yield: 4 servings.

STEWED MIXED FRUITS

1 small stick cinnamon
¾ teaspoon whole cloves
½ (8-ounce) package dried prunes
½ (8-ounce) package dried apples
½ (6-ounce) package dried apricots
3 cups water
¼ cup firmly packed brown sugar

Place cinnamon and cloves in a cheesecloth bag; tie bag, and place in a saucepan. Add remaining ingredients; bring to a boil. Reduce heat; simmer 30 minutes. Cool slightly; discard spice bag. Serve warm. Yield: 4 to 6 servings.

BROILED CORNISH HENS

4 (2- to 2½-pound) Cornish hens
2 tablespoons salt
1 tablespoon pepper
¼ cup butter or margarine, softened
Watercress

Remove giblets from hens; discard. Rinse hens with cold water, and pat dry. Split hens down backs, and open flat; lay hens, breast side down, on a lightly greased rack in a shallow roasting pan. Rub with butter. Sprinkle with salt and pepper.

Broil hens 5 inches from heating element 10 minutes on each side or until drumsticks move easily. Transfer hens to a warm serving platter; garnish with watercress. Serve immediately. Yield: 4 servings.

BAKED TOMATO HALVES

2 large tomatoes
¼ cup fine, dry breadcrumbs
1½ tablespoons butter or margarine, melted
½ teaspoon garlic powder
¾ teaspoon ground coriander
¾ teaspoon ground cumin
½ teaspoon seasoned salt
Chopped fresh parsley (optional)

Remove cores from tomatoes; cut each tomato in half crosswise. Arrange tomatoes in a shallow 1-quart baking dish.

Combine breadcrumbs, butter, and seasonings in a small mixing bowl; mix well. Spread 1 tablespoon of breadcrumb mixture over cut surface of each tomato. Cover with plastic wrap; refrigerate overnight.

Remove plastic wrap, and let tomatoes stand at room temperature 10 minutes. Bake, uncovered, at 350° for 25 minutes or until topping is golden brown. Garnish each tomato half with chopped parsley, if desired, before serving. Serve warm. Yield: 4 servings.

PECAN LOAF

1 cup milk
1 package dry yeast
1 tablespoon sugar
3 cups all-purpose flour, divided
2 tablespoons butter or margarine, softened
⅓ cup sugar
1 egg white
1 cup chopped pecans
¼ teaspoon salt
Cream cheese (optional)

Scald milk; let cool to lukewarm (105° to 115°). Dissolve yeast and 1 tablespoon sugar in warm milk in a large mixing bowl; stirring well. Let stand 5 minutes or until bubbly.

Add 1 cup flour, beating until smooth. Cover and let rise in a warm place (85°), free from drafts, 45 minutes or until doubled in bulk.

Cream butter in a large mixing bowl; gradually add ⅓ cup sugar, beating well.

Beat egg white (at room temperature) until stiff peaks form. Stir egg white, pecans, salt, yeast mixture, and remaining flour into creamed mixture to make a soft dough.

Turn dough out onto a floured surface. Knead 8 minutes or until smooth and elastic. Place dough in a greased bowl, turning to grease top. Cover and repeat rising procedure 1½ hours or until doubled in bulk.

Punch dough down; turn out onto a lightly floured surface, and shape into a loaf. Place in a well-greased 9- x 5- x 3-inch loaf-pan. Cover and repeat rising procedure 1 hour or until doubled in bulk.

Bake at 325° for 15 minutes; increase temperature to 350°, and bake an additional 30 minutes or until loaf sounds hollow when tapped. Remove bread from pan immediately, and cool on a wire rack. Slice loaf, and serve with cream cheese, if desired. Yield: 1 loaf.

MORNING CALL

T he season of the year has less bearing on our breakfast planning than it once did. Of greater influence, now that fresh pork and strawberries, for example, are available all year, is Southern geography. A Baltimorian breakfasting in San Antonio will discover a whole new way to treat his taste buds when he cauterizes them with ranchero sauce inflamed with chili. Shad roe was never like this!

But shad roe is historically and currently a seasonal delicacy. This spring tonic of Maryland and Virginia is as eagerly awaited as the first asparagus in the garden. Folks on this part of the coast will have none of the Florida roe available in winter. They swear the roe is fatter and rosier-hued after the shad has migrated north and entered the local rivers. This is the same shad roe that was once so commonplace that the well-to-do shunned it, lest they be thought poor.

Time was, a fresh pork breakfast could be had only at the first real cold snap, when it was safe to butcher. By this time in late fall, nearly everyone would have run out of cured ham and bacon. Today's palate, honed on instant gratification, cannot imagine how wonderful that first "mess" of fresh meat tasted, any more than we can feel the heavenly warmth of the wood stove that cooked it. Few people can now recall the self-sustaining farm complete with bee hives, where " . . . breakfasts were especially bountiful: fruit in season, scrambled eggs, fried ham, shoulder or sausage in the wintertime; bacon in the summer. Often fried apples and always hot buckwheat biscuits and honey. . . ."

"Let glad Shrove Tuesday bring the pancake thin, or fritter rich, with apples stored within." The custom of eating pancakes on Shrove Tuesday was already old in 1445, when the women of Olney, England, started their annual pancake race, flipping the cakes as they ran. The tradition continues, and people in other countries imitate it. Pancakes and related recipes cooked on a griddle accompanied by special syrups make a satisfying and easy meal.

Shrimp for breakfast seems the ultimate luxury to an inlander or any visitor unaccustomed to it. What else do we serve for a special breakfast? Just about anything we please; the menu is limited only by the imagination.

MENU OF MENUS

MARYLAND SPRING
BREAKFAST FOR TWO

WINTER FARM
BREAKFAST

EARLY MORNING IN THE
FRENCH QUARTER

PANCAKE BREAKFAST

MEXICAN BREAKFAST

BREAKFAST WITH A
FISHERMAN

In the seaboard tradition: Shad Roe with Bacon, fresh strawberries with cream, Cornmeal Muffins, and coffee. Photographed in the kitchen of the Hammond-Harwood House, Annapolis, Maryland.

MARYLAND SPRING BREAKFAST FOR TWO

Marylanders and others living within seafood range of the Chesapeake Bay know when spring arrives, no matter if the weather seems inclement: Shad roe come on the market as surely as crocus push through snow. And that's when everyone suddenly wants nothing but shad roe for breakfast, preferably with a "side" of asparagus, that other gastronomic harbinger of the season of renewal. Strawberries are in the market too, though they come from further south; nobody needs to be persuaded to eat them by the bowlful, with sweet cream poured over with a heavy hand. In cooking shad roe, it is well to remember that overcooking toughens — have a care!

FRESH STRAWBERRIES WITH CREAM
SHAD ROE WITH BACON
FRESH ASPARAGUS
CORNMEAL MUFFINS

Serves 2

SHAD ROE WITH BACON

8 slices bacon, halved
1 medium onion, cut into thick slices and separated into rings
3 tablespoons all-purpose flour
¼ teaspoon salt
¼ teaspoon lemon-pepper seasoning
⅛ teaspoon garlic powder
⅛ teaspoon onion powder
2 pair small shad roe
2 tablespoons lemon juice

Cook bacon in a large skillet until crisp; drain well, reserving bacon drippings in skillet. Set bacon aside.

Sauté onion rings in reserved drippings until tender. Remove skillet from heat; set aside.

Combine flour and spices in a shallow pan. Carefully rinse shad roe, and sprinkle with lemon juice; dredge in flour mixture. Place roe in skillet with sautéed onion. Cover and cook over medium-high heat 5 minutes or until roe is no longer red. Transfer roe to individual serving plates. Arrange bacon and onion slices over top. Serve hot. Yield: 2 servings.

FRESH ASPARAGUS

½ pound fresh asparagus spears
2 tablespoons butter or margarine, melted
Lemon wedges

Snap off tough ends of asparagus. Remove scales from stalks with a knife or vegetable peeler, if desired. Tie asparagus into a bundle with kitchen string.

Stand bundle, tips up, on rack in the bottom of a double boiler. Add boiling water to a depth of 1 inch. Cover with top of double boiler, turned upside down for a lid. Simmer 10 minutes or until desired degree. of doneness. Drain asparagus well. Cut and remove string.

Arrange asparagus spears on a serving platter. Drizzle butter over asparagus. Serve with lemon wedges. Yield: 2 servings.

Asparagus at its freshest, with lemon and butter.

Historic Hammond-Harwood House at Annapolis, Maryland. The well-furnished kitchen interior (top) and the classic facade (below).

CORNMEAL MUFFINS

1¼ cups cornmeal
¼ cup all-purpose flour
1½ teaspoons baking powder
¼ teaspoon baking soda
½ teaspoon salt
1 egg, beaten
1 cup buttermilk
2 tablespoons shortening, melted

Combine first 5 ingredients in a medium mixing bowl; make a well in center of mixture. Combine egg, buttermilk, and shortening; mix well. Add to dry ingredients, stirring just until moistened.

Heat a well-greased muffin pan in a 400° oven 3 minutes or until very hot. Spoon mixture into muffin pan, filling two-thirds full. Bake at 450° for 18 minutes or until lightly browned. Yield: 10 muffins.

Late Snow in Georgia, *by folk artist Mattie Lou O'Kelley*

WINTER FARM BREAKFAST

A different scene altogether from the plantation breakfast at nine or ten o'clock preceded by an early "dram," was the breakfast at dawn on the middle-class, self-sustaining working farms that evolved later. Food processing consumed most of a woman's waking hours, what with gardening, canning, drying, and bread-making, in addition to producing one rib-sticking meal after another, with little respite in between. She accepted whatever help was to be had from older children and possibly a "hired girl." Cold weather and hog-butchering time meant feverish activity — and the best breakfasts of the year. Fresh pork with gravy and biscuits has yet to be supplanted as the Southerner's favorite winter breakfast.

PORK CHOPS WITH CREAM GRAVY
SCRAMBLED EGGS
FRIED MUSH
STEWED PRUNES
SELF-RISING BISCUITS
MOLASSES

Serves 6

PORK CHOPS WITH CREAM GRAVY

½ cup cracker meal
1 teaspoon poultry seasoning
¼ teaspoon salt
⅛ teaspoon pepper
6 (½-inch-thick) pork chops
2 tablespoons bacon drippings
1 tablespoon all-purpose flour
1 cup milk, scalded
Salt and pepper to taste
Fresh parsley sprigs (optional)
Spiced crabapples (optional)

Combine cracker meal, poultry seasoning, ¼ teaspoon salt, and ⅛ teaspoon pepper in a medium mixing bowl; mix well. Dredge pork chops in cracker meal mixture.

Heat bacon drippings in a 10-inch skillet over high heat. Cook chops 4 minutes on each side or until browned. Drain on paper towels, reserving drippings in skillet. Transfer chops to a serving platter; keep warm.

Add flour to pan drippings, stirring until well blended. Cook over medium heat, stirring constantly, 1 minute. Gradually add scalded milk; cook over medium heat, stirring constantly, until thickened and bubbly. Stir in salt and pepper to taste. Pour gravy into serving bowl.

Garnish pork chops with parsley sprigs and crabapples, if desired. Serve immediately with gravy. Yield: 6 servings.

SCRAMBLED EGGS

12 eggs
⅔ cup whipping cream
½ teaspoon salt
¼ teaspoon pepper
¼ cup butter or margarine

Combine eggs, whipping cream, salt, and pepper in a large mixing bowl; beat with a wire whisk until well blended.

Melt butter in a large skillet over medium heat; add egg mixture. Cook over medium heat, stirring occasionally, until eggs are set. Serve immediately. Yield: 6 servings.

FRIED MUSH

1½ cups yellow cornmeal
½ cup plus 3 tablespoons all-purpose flour, divided
1½ teaspoons salt
1½ cups cold water
4½ cups water
Vegetable oil

Combine cornmeal, 3 tablespoons flour, and salt in a medium mixing bowl. Add 1½ cups cold water, stirring until well blended.

Bring 4½ cups water to a boil in a large Dutch oven; add cornmeal mixture, stirring until well blended. Reduce heat; simmer 10 minutes, stirring frequently. Pour mixture into a lightly greased 15- x 10- x 1-inch jellyroll pan. Cover and refrigerate overnight.

Cut mush into 3- x 2-inch pieces; dredge in remaining flour. Fry in hot oil (375°) in a large skillet, a few pieces at a time, turning occasionally until golden brown on both sides. Drain well on paper towels. Serve warm. Yield: 6 servings.

STEWED PRUNES

1½ (24-ounce) packages dried, pitted prunes
4 slices lemon
4 (4-inch) sticks cinnamon
1 cup plus 2 tablespoons sugar

Place prunes with water to cover in a small saucepan; let stand 30 minutes, and drain. Return prunes to saucepan with water to cover. Add lemon slices and cinnamon; bring to a boil. Reduce heat; cover and cook 20 minutes or until prunes begin to swell. Add sugar, and continue cooking 10 minutes.

Remove prunes; place in a 1-quart serving bowl, and set aside. Continue cooking juice 15 minutes or until thickened. Pour over reserved prunes, discarding lemon slices and cinnamon sticks. Cover and chill thoroughly. Spoon into individual serving dishes, and serve cold. Yield: 6 servings.

SELF-RISING BISCUITS

4 cups self-rising flour
1 cup shortening
1½ cups milk

Place flour in a large mixing bowl. Cut in shortening with a pastry blender until mixture resembles coarse meal. Gradually add milk, stirring until flour mixture is moistened.

Turn dough out onto a lightly floured surface, and knead 4 to 5 times.

Roll dough to ¾-inch thickness; cut with a 3-inch biscuit cutter. Place on a lightly greased baking sheet. Bake at 450° for 10 minutes or until lightly browned. Yield: 1 dozen.

Cold weather breakfast of Pork Chops, Cream Gravy, Self-Rising Biscuits, and molasses.

EARLY MORNING IN THE FRENCH QUARTER

The market district in New Orleans' French Quarter awakens long before dawn and quickly fills with working folks on their way to their jobs, stopping off for a very special eye-opener: the traditional café au lait with sugared beignets (French doughnuts). This custom is a continuation of an ancient French day starter, the *petit déjeuner*, or little breakfast. The early work force in line for their energizing snack find themselves in the company of revelers winding up a night on the town.

 BEIGNETS
CAFÉ AU LAIT

Serves 12

Say "Good Morning!" with Beignets and Café au Lait

BEIGNETS

¼ cup sugar
2 tablespoons shortening
½ teaspoon salt
½ cup boiling water
½ cup evaporated milk
½ package dry yeast
¼ cup lukewarm water (105° to 115°)
1 egg, beaten
3½ to 3¾ cups all-purpose flour, divided
Vegetable oil
Sifted powdered sugar

Place sugar, shortening, and salt in a large mixing bowl; add boiling water and milk, stirring well. Let cool to lukewarm (105° to 115°).

Dissolve yeast in lukewarm water, stirring well. Let stand 5 minutes or until bubbly. Add dissolved yeast and egg to lukewarm milk mixture, stirring until well blended. Add 2 cups flour; beat well. Stir in enough remaining flour to make a soft dough. Cover and refrigerate overnight.

Turn dough out onto a floured surface; roll to ⅛-inch thickness. Cut into 2-inch squares. Drop squares, a few at a time, into deep hot oil (375°). Fry until golden brown, turning once. Drain on paper towels.

Place powdered sugar in a paper bag; place 2 to 3 beignets in bag, and shake well. Repeat procedure with remaining beignets; serve immediately. Yield: about 3½ dozen.

French Market coffee stand from Frank Leslie's Illustrated Newspaper, *1883.*

Coffee label, c.1915.

CAFÉ AU LAIT

¾ cup drip grind coffee and chickory
6 cups boiling water
6 cups milk
Sugar to taste (optional)

Place coffee grounds in basket of a French drip coffee pot. Pour boiling water, 2 tablespoons at a time, over coffee grounds. Continue process until all water has dripped through grounds.

Bring milk to a boil.

To serve, pour ½ cup coffee and ½ cup milk in a serving cup. Add sugar to taste, if desired, stirring well. Serve immediately. Yield: 12 cups.

PANCAKE BREAKFAST

From the "pancake thin" of Shrove Tuesday and other references, we might assume that "thin, thinner, thinnest" was the rule for early pancakes. An old Lee family recipe from Arlington was for thin, French crêpe-style pancakes called "Quire of Paper," served with maple sugar in between, and cut into wedges. Mary Randolph, a kinswoman of the Lees and author of *The Virginia Housewife*, 1824, made her "Quire of Paper Pancakes" with wine and advised the reader to ". . . run them as thin as possible, and when coloured, they are done. . . . Do not turn them, but lay them carefully in the dish, sprinkling powdered sugar between each layer." It was later that Southerners accented the pancake by adding grits and rice to the batter, making a hefty cake to stack and serve with corn syrup poured over the top.

BASIC PANCAKES
BREADCRUMB PANCAKES
CORNMEAL PANCAKES
BLUEBERRY PANCAKES
POTATO GRIDDLE CAKES
APPLE FRITTERS
BLUEBERRY SAUCE

BASIC PANCAKES

2 cups all purpose flour
2 tablespoons sugar
1 tablespoon plus 1 teaspoon
   baking powder
½ teaspoon salt
1⅓ cups milk
1 egg, beaten
2 tablespoons butter or
   margarine, melted

Combine flour, sugar, baking powder, and salt in a large mixing bowl. Combine milk and egg, mixing well; slowly stir into dry ingredients. Gradually add butter to batter, stirring well.

For each pancake, pour ¼ cup batter onto a hot, lightly greased griddle. Cook until tops of pancakes are covered with bubbles and edges appear slightly dry. Turn and continue cooking until bottom sides are browned. Serve with butter and syrup. Yield: twelve 4-inch pancakes.

Basic Pancakes can be dressed up with real butter and almost any sweet topping. Blueberry Sauce is a favorite.

BREADCRUMB PANCAKES

1 cup fine, dry breadcrumbs
2 tablespoons sugar
1½ teaspoons baking
  powder
¼ teaspoon salt
2 eggs, beaten
1 cup milk
½ cup commercial sour
  cream

Combine breadcrumbs, sugar, baking powder, and salt in a medium mixing bowl; mix well. Combine eggs, milk, and sour cream in a small mixing bowl, stirring until smooth. Add egg mixture to dry ingredients, mixing just until moistened.

Drop batter by tablespoonfuls onto a hot, lightly greased griddle or skillet. Cook until tops of pancakes are covered with bubbles and edges appear slightly dry. Turn and continue cooking until bottom sides are browned. Serve hot with butter and syrup. Yield: 2 dozen 2-inch pancakes.

CORNMEAL PANCAKES

2 cups cornmeal
1 cup all-purpose flour
1 tablespoon sugar
1 teaspoon baking
  powder
½ teaspoon baking
  soda
1 teaspoon salt
3½ cups buttermilk
2 eggs, beaten

Combine cornmeal, flour, sugar, baking powder, soda, and salt in a medium mixing bowl. Combine buttermilk and eggs; slowly stir mixture into dry ingredients.

For each pancake, pour ¼ cup batter onto a hot, lightly greased griddle. Cook until tops of pancakes are covered with bubbles and edges appear slightly dry. Turn and continue cooking until bottom sides are browned. Serve hot with butter and syrup. Yield: about 2 dozen 4-inch pancakes.

Trade card for Heckers' Buckwheat, 1893.

BLUEBERRY PANCAKES

2 cups all-purpose flour
2 tablespoons sugar
1 tablespoon baking powder
1 teaspoon salt
1½ cups milk
2 eggs, beaten
3 tablespoons butter or
  margarine, melted
1 (16½-ounce) can
  blueberries, drained

Combine dry ingredients in a mixing bowl. Combine milk, eggs, and butter; stir into dry ingredients. Fold in blueberries.

For each pancake, pour ¼ cup batter onto a hot, lightly greased griddle. Cook until tops are covered with bubbles and edges appear slightly dry. Turn and cook until bottom sides are browned. Serve hot with butter and syrup. Yield: about twelve 4-inch pancakes.

POTATO GRIDDLE CAKES

2 cups all-purpose flour
⅓ cup cornmeal
1 tablespoon sugar
1 tablespoon baking powder
2 teaspoons salt
2 eggs, beaten
1¾ cups milk
½ cup cold, cooked mashed
  potatoes
⅓ cup shortening, melted

Combine first 5 ingredients in a medium mixing bowl; stir well. Combine eggs, milk, potatoes, and shortening; beat well. Stir into dry ingredients.

For each pancake, pour ¼ cup batter onto a hot, lightly greased griddle. Cook until tops are covered with bubbles and edges are slightly dry. Turn and cook until bottom sides are browned. Serve with butter and syrup. Yield: sixteen 4-inch pancakes.

Colorful manufacturer's label for Okatoma Brand Pure Cane Syrup, a product of Sanford, Mississippi, 1906.

APPLE FRITTERS

⅔ cup milk
2 eggs, separated
1 tablespoon butter or
    margarine, melted
1¼ cups all-purpose flour
¼ cup sugar, divided
¼ teaspoon salt
2½ cups peeled, diced
    cooking apples
½ cup chopped pecans
Vegetable oil
Sifted powdered sugar

Combine milk, egg yolks, and butter in a medium mixing bowl, beating well. Combine flour, 1 tablespoon sugar, and salt in a small mixing bowl, stirring until well blended; gradually fold into egg yolk mixture. Cover and refrigerate 2 hours.

Sprinkle remaining 3 tablespoons sugar over diced apples;

toss gently, and set aside.

Beat egg whites (at room temperature) until stiff peaks form. Gently fold beaten egg whites into chilled batter. Fold chopped apple mixture and pecans into fritter batter.

Heat ½ inch oil in a large skillet to 375°; drop mixture by tablespoonfuls into hot oil. Cook 1 minute on each side or until golden brown. Drain on paper towels. Sprinkle with powdered sugar. Yield: about 2 dozen.

BLUEBERRY SAUCE

1½ cups sugar
1 cup water
2 tablespoons lemon
    juice
2 cups fresh or frozen
    blueberries, divided (thaw,
    if frozen)

Combine sugar, water, and lemon juice in a heavy saucepan. Bring mixture to a boil; cook 8 minutes. Add 1 cup blueberries, and boil 5 minutes. Cool mixture slightly. Add remaining blueberries, stirring well. Serve sauce warm over pancakes or waffles. Yield: about 2½ cups.

MEXICAN BREAKFAST

It would be unrealistic to look for a meal in the Southwest that did not in some way betray the underlying Spanish-Mexican background of the food. As prevalent as cowboy boots and ten-gallon hats, there is always the forthright regionality of the food to make us aware of pride of heritage. Expect, for example, breakfast or brunch in a private home to include one or more of the following: Huevos Rancheros with tortillas or rice and Mexican Sauce, Chorizo, the chili-seasoned Mexican sausage, and Frijoles, popular at any meal, not excepting breakfast. Then there's Café con Leche, akin to the French Café au Lait, but spicier—with cloves, cinnamon, and cardamom.

MEXICAN BLOODY MARY
CHORIZO
HUEVOS RANCHEROS
FRIJOLES
CHILE-CHEESE RICE
MANGO SALAD
CAFÉ CON LECHE

Serves 8

MEXICAN BLOODY MARY

1 (46-ounce) can tomato juice
1½ cups tequila
1 teaspoon Worcestershire sauce
¾ teaspoon hot sauce
¾ teaspoon onion juice

Combine all ingredients, mixing well. Pour into a large pitcher. Serve in glasses over ice. Yield: about 7 cups.

CHORIZO

1 clove garlic
1 tablespoon dried whole oregano
½ cup chili powder
½ cup vinegar
½ cup water
2 pounds ground pork

Combine garlic, oregano, chili powder, vinegar, and water in the container of an electric blender; process until mixture is well blended. Place ground meat in a large mixing bowl; pour sauce over top of meat. Cover and refrigerate mixture overnight.

Drain meat mixture through a colander, discarding any liquid. Crumble meat mixture into a large skillet, and cook over medium heat, stirring occasionally, until meat is browned. Drain well. Transfer sausage to a serving platter, and serve warm. Yield: 8 servings.

Rugged cowboy is suitable symbol for J. S. McManus Produce Co. of Texas, 1940.

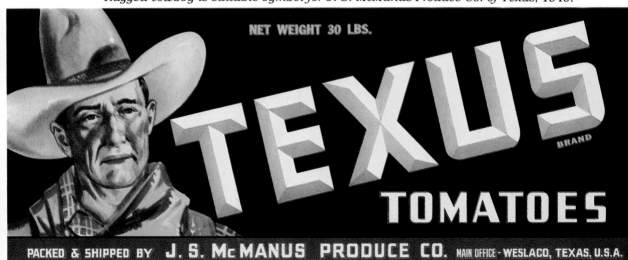

SMALL RED CHILI PEPPER

HUEVOS RANCHEROS

8 corn tortillas
Vegetable oil
8 eggs
Mexican Sauce
Grated Monterey Jack cheese

Fry tortillas in hot oil until crisp but not browned; drain on paper towels. Place tortillas on baking sheets, and set aside.

Fry each egg in a small amount of hot oil until eggs are set. Top each tortilla with a fried egg; spoon 2 tablespoons Mexican Sauce over top. Sprinkle with grated cheese. Broil just until cheese melts.

Transfer to a serving platter, and serve immediately. Yield: 8 servings.

Mexican Sauce:

1 clove garlic, minced
1½ teaspoons salt
1 small onion, finely chopped
2 tablespoons olive oil
4 (8-ounce) cans tomato sauce
1 (10½-ounce) can beef consommé, undiluted
½ (4-ounce) can chopped green chiles, undrained
½ teaspoon ground cumin

Place garlic in a large heavy skillet; sprinkle with salt, and mash well with the back of a spoon to combine. Add onion and olive oil; sauté until onion is transparent. Stir in tomato sauce, beef consommé, chiles, and cumin. Bring to a boil; reduce heat. Simmer, uncovered, 30 minutes, stirring occasionally. Cover and refrigerate overnight. Serve at room temperature. Yield: 1 quart.

FRIJOLES

1 (16-ounce) package dried pinto beans
7 cups water
1 pound salt pork, diced
1 small onion, sliced
2 cloves garlic, sliced
2 teaspoons sugar

Sort and wash beans; place in a large Dutch oven. Cover with water 2 inches above beans; let soak overnight.

Drain beans; cover with 7 cups water. Stir in remaining ingredients. Bring to a boil. Reduce heat; simmer, uncovered, 3 hours or until beans are tender. Spoon into a serving bowl. Yield: 8 servings.

CHILE-CHEESE RICE

3 cups hot cooked rice
1 (16-ounce) carton commercial sour cream
¼ teaspoon salt
1 (8-ounce) package Monterey Jack cheese, cubed
2 (4-ounce) cans chopped green chiles, undrained
½ cup (2 ounces) shredded Monterey Jack cheese

Combine rice, sour cream, and salt in a medium mixing bowl; stir well. Spoon one-third of rice mixture into a buttered 2-quart casserole.

Layer half each of cubed cheese and green chiles on top; repeat layers with rice mixture, cubed cheese, and chiles, ending with remaining rice mixture. Sprinkle shredded cheese over top. Bake at 350° for 30 minutes or until thoroughly heated and cheese melts. Serve hot. Yield: 8 servings.

MANGO SALAD

2 (15-ounce) cans mangos, undrained
3 cups water
3 (3-ounce) packages lemon-flavored gelatin
1 (8-ounce) package cream cheese, softened
2 tablespoons lime juice
Grated coconut

Drain mangos, reserving juice. Set mangos aside. Combine mango juice and water in a medium saucepan; bring to a boil. Add gelatin, and stir until gelatin dissolves; remove from heat, and cool slightly.

Combine mangos and cream cheese in container of an electric blender; process until smooth. Add to gelatin mixture, mixing well. Stir in lime juice. Pour mixture into a lightly greased 8-cup mold. Cover and chill overnight.

Unmold onto a serving platter. Garnish with coconut. Yield: 8 servings.

CAFÉ CON LECHE

¾ cup firmly packed dark brown sugar
2 tablespoons water
6 whole cloves
1 (2-inch) stick cinnamon
⅛ teaspoon ground cardamom
Pinch of salt
6 cups strong hot coffee
2 cups half-and-half

Combine first 6 ingredients in a small saucepan. Bring to a boil, stirring until sugar dissolves. Add sugar mixture to hot coffee; cover and let steep 15 minutes. Strain coffee mixture into a serving pot.

Heat half-and-half to just below boiling; stir into coffee mixture. Yield: 8½ cups.

Huevos Rancheros and Chorizo are surrounded by Mexican Sauce, Mango Salad, Mexican Bloody Marys, Chile-Cheese Rice, and Frijoles.

BREAKFAST WITH A FISHERMAN

nyone who loves the outdoors and freshly fried fish will positively jump at the chance to breakfast with an avid fisherman. However, there are those who like being outdoors but have no ambition to wet a line. These folks are not asked to breakfast with a fisherman unless they know how to (1) build cookfires (or man a 2-burner camp stove) and (2) cook potatoes and hush puppies. In all fairness, the one who catches them has his hands full, skinning and filleting a mess of "cats," and should be excused from the remaining preparations. One solution: Offer to go along for the ride, then bring the dressed fish back to your place. Now, pull out the skillet and deep-fryer and treat that fisherman to the best fish breakfast he ever sank his teeth into. You can even serve the breakfast on enamel-ware to make him feel "at camp."

FRESH APPLES OR BLUEBERRIES
FRIED CATFISH FILLETS
SHOE-STRING POTATOES
GOLDEN HUSH PUPPIES
RIVERBANK COFFEE

Serves 6

FRIED CATFISH FILLETS

2 pounds catfish fillets
1 teaspoon salt
¼ teaspoon pepper
2 cups self-rising cornmeal
Vegetable oil

Sprinkle fish with salt and pepper; dredge in cornmeal. Carefully drop fish into deep hot oil (375°). Fry until fish float to the top and are golden brown; drain well. Serve hot. Yield: 6 servings.

SHOE-STRING POTATOES

4 large potatoes, washed, peeled, and cut into long, thin strips
Vegetable oil
Salt and pepper to taste

Soak potatoes in cold water to cover at least 30 minutes. Drain well and pat dry.

Cook potatoes in deep hot oil (375°) until golden brown and crispy. Drain on paper towels. Sprinkle with salt and pepper. Serve hot. Yield: 6 servings.

Catfish fillets, Shoe-String Potatoes, and hush puppies.

Camping in the Woods/A Good Time Coming, *by Currier and Ives, 1863.*

GOLDEN HUSH PUPPIES

2 cups self-rising cornmeal
1 small onion,
   finely chopped
1 cup milk
2 eggs, beaten
Vegetable oil

Combine cornmeal and onion in a medium mixing bowl. Add milk and egg, stirring well.

Drop batter by tablespoonfuls into deep hot oil (375°), cooking only a few at a time. Cook 2 minutes; turn and cook an additional 2 minutes or until hush puppies are golden brown. Drain well on paper towels. Serve hot. Yield: about 2 dozen.

RIVERBANK COFFEE

2 quarts cold water
1 cup regular grind coffee
1 egg, beaten
2 tablespoons water
Dash of salt
½ cup cold water

Bring 2 quarts cold water to a boil in a large pot. Combine coffee, egg, 2 tablespoons water, and salt in a small bowl; stir well. Stir coffee mixture into boiling water. Return to a boil, stirring occasionally. Remove from heat; pour ½ cup cold water over coffee mixture to settle grounds. Let stand 10 minutes. Serve hot in coffee mugs. Yield: 8 cups.

The on-site fish breakfast usually takes place during a camping or hiking trip. Equipment has to be planned carefully, weight being the chief consideration if hiking with backpacks for any length of time. Skillets, except for a lightweight, nonstick one, are left behind, along with oil for frying. Backpackers use bacon drippings, no deep-frying. If limited to one pan, cook fish first, then potatoes, then hush puppies.

FROM TEN 'TIL NOON

*Breakfast breads need only
fruit and coffee to make
a memorable brunch:
Swedish Tea Ring (front),
Apple Roll (left), Croissants
(top), and Cinnamon Rolls.*

The second breakfast, after the day's work was initiated, was indulged in by planters and others with leisure. The bracing julep or that quick cup of coffee with cold bread and snippets of yesterday's roast did not pack enough energy to last until three o'clock dinner. Hot bread and meat, later in the morning, were served with eggs, fruit, preserves, and, on the coast, seafood.

Hostesses began parlaying the second breakfast into a company affair before the turn of the century. Arbiters of taste were writing prolifically about correct procedures, and food writers backed them up with menus that would give a modern party-giver prostrations. This meal ". . . is very much in favor with people of the leisure class, and also with the artist and *littérateur*, who frequently have considerable time to kill. . . ." The time was set as between ten and noon, not to "infringe upon the hours appointed by custom for luncheons."

The breakfast we now celebrate as brunch, in elegant homes, could run to seven courses. The fifth course in a "winter breakfast menu" in *Practical Cooking and Dinner Giving* by Mary F. Henderson (1877) was "Fillets of Grouse (each fillet cut in two) on little thin slices of fried mush, garnished with potatoes Parisienne." Could the male guests, correctly attired in morning dress, distinguish between mush and potatoes at this point? Could the women in street costume (not removing their hats) last all the way through the *dénouement*, waffles with maple syrup?

In evolving the modern brunch, we've dropped the pretensions and gone largely to buffet-style service. Our scaled-down menus can be accomplished without an army of helpers. We make a point of timing a brunch for a weekend or holiday when everyone can feel he has "time to kill."

Categorically cooking, sweet yeast breads can be impressive and not hard to make, once we understand that any yeast dough can well take its first rising overnight in the refrigerator. Guests tend to think yeast baking much more trouble than it is, so go ahead and impress them with your own pastry sampler!

Here are recipes to serve from ten 'til noon, including workable facsimiles of some old-time extravaganzas.

BREAKFAST PASTRY SAMPLER

Looked at one way, this segment contains several great recipes, any one of which could light up a breakfast menu. Overnight rolls and breads are not new; old-time housewives knew that cool air retards yeast growth and used the fact to fit yeast baking into an otherwise tight schedule. Putting a bowl of dough in a cool place at bedtime and letting it sit overnight resulted in a nice, risen mass ready for shaping at dawn. That lady's timing was such that just as the early chores were finished, she could take a fragrant sweet bread from the oven, like a rabbit from a hat. Another thought is this: Invite some friends. The night before, make lots of your favorite sweet yeast dough and use that one dough to make cinnamon rolls, apple rolls, and a tea ring. Such sleight of hand will wow the audience. Have lots of coffee.

CROISSANTS
GLAZED DOUGHNUTS
APPLE ROLL
SWEDISH TEA RING
CINNAMON ROLLS
RED PLUM JAM
APPLE BUTTER

CROISSANTS

1 cup butter, softened
⅔ cup milk
2 packages dry yeast
3 tablespoons sugar, divided
½ cup lukewarm water (105° to 115°)
4 to 4½ cups all-purpose flour, divided
¼ cup vegetable oil
2 teaspoons salt
2 eggs, beaten

Stir butter with a wooden spoon until smooth; spread on waxed paper into a 10- x 8-inch rectangle. Chill until needed.

Scald milk; cool to 105° to 115°. Dissolve yeast and 1 tablespoon sugar in lukewarm water in a large mixing bowl; let stand 5 minutes or until bubbly. Stir in lukewarm milk, 2 cups flour, oil, remaining sugar, salt, and eggs; beat at medium speed of an electric mixer until smooth. Gradually stir in enough remaining flour to make a soft dough.

Turn dough out onto a floured surface; knead 10 minutes or until smooth and elastic. Place dough in a well-greased bowl, turning to grease top. Cover and let rise in a warm place (85°), free from drafts, 1 hour or until doubled in bulk.

Punch dough down. Cover with plastic wrap, and refrigerate 1 hour.

Punch dough down, and turn out onto a lightly floured surface; roll into a 24- x 10-inch rectangle. Place chilled butter rectangle on half of dough. Fold other half of dough over butter to form a 12- x 10-inch rectangle; pinch edges to seal.

Roll dough into an 18- x 10-inch rectangle. Fold into thirds, beginning with short side. Cover and chill 1 hour.

Repeat rolling and folding procedure (roll into an 18- x 10-inch rectangle, and fold into thirds) 2 additional times, covering and chilling dough 30 minutes between procedures. Wrap dough in aluminum foil, and chill overnight.

Divide dough into 4 equal portions; chill 3 portions. Roll 1 portion into a 12-inch circle on a lightly floured surface; cut into 6 wedges. Roll up each wedge tightly, beginning at wide end. Seal points, and place point side down on greased baking sheets; curve into crescent shapes. Cover and repeat rising procedure 30 minutes or until doubled in bulk.

Bake at 425° for 8 minutes or until golden brown. Cool slightly on baking sheets, and transfer to wire racks to cool completely. Repeat shaping, rising, baking, and cooling procedures with remaining dough portions. Yield: 2 dozen.

Note: Croissants may also be served warm.

Meltingly tender Glazed Doughnuts (and holes) go with milk or coffee for a satisfying snack.

GLAZED DOUGHNUTS

2 packages dry yeast
¼ cup plus 1 teaspoon sugar, divided
½ cup lukewarm water (105° to 115°)
1 cup milk, scalded
1 teaspoon salt
¼ cup plus 2 tablespoons shortening
4¼ cups all-purpose flour
Vegetable oil
Glaze (recipe follows)

Dissolve yeast and 1 teaspoon sugar in water in a small bowl, stirring well; let stand 5 minutes or until bubbly.

Combine milk, remaining sugar, salt, and shortening in a large mixing bowl, stirring until shortening melts. Cool to lukewarm (105° to 115°).

Add yeast mixture to milk mixture; stir well. Add flour, stirring to make a soft dough.

Place dough in a lightly greased bowl, turning to grease top. Cover and let rise in a warm place (85°), free from drafts, 45 minutes or until dough is doubled in bulk.

Punch dough down. Turn out onto a lightly floured surface; let rest 5 minutes. Roll to ½-inch thickness; cut with a floured doughnut cutter. Place doughnuts and holes on greased baking sheets. Cover and repeat rising procedure 30 minutes or until doubled in bulk.

Drop doughnuts and holes, a few at a time, into deep hot oil (375°). Fry until golden brown, turning once. Drain well. Dip doughnuts in glaze. Serve hot. Yield: about 2 dozen.

Glaze:

⅓ cup boiling water
2 cups sifted powdered sugar

Combine water and sugar, mixing well until sugar dissolves. Keep warm. Yield: about 1¾ cups.

Some years back, archaeologists working an ancient Indian site in the Southwest unearthed some petrified cakes that had been fried and had holes in the middle. Were they doughnuts? Or merely proof that a primitive woman had the practical notion that a hot cake with a hole in it would be easier to pick up with her cooking stick? It was the Dutch settlers who brought the doughnut to the Northeast, and the hole is there because it promotes even cooking. Southerners referred to doughnuts as "Yankee cakes."

Picking and packing the apple crop in Nelson County, Virginia, c.1920.

APPLE ROLL

1 package dry yeast
1 cup milk, scalded, cooled to 105° to 115°, and divided
4 cups all-purpose flour
½ cup sugar, divided
1 teaspoon salt
1 cup shortening
2 eggs, beaten
½ cup butter or margarine, melted
4 cooking apples, peeled, cored, and thinly sliced
1 cup firmly packed brown sugar
1 cup flaked coconut
1 cup pecans, finely chopped
2 teaspoons ground cinnamon
Cinnamon Glaze

Dissolve yeast in ¼ cup milk, stirring well; set aside.

Sift together flour, ¼ cup sugar, and salt in a large mixing bowl; cut in shortening with a pastry blender. Add remaining milk, eggs, and yeast mixture to flour mixture; stir well. Cover; refrigerate overnight.

Turn dough out onto a lightly floured surface; divide into 4 equal portions. Roll each portion into a rectangle ¼-inch-thick on a floured pastry cloth; brush each with butter. Arrange apple slices evenly over rectangles. Sprinkle each with one-fourth of brown sugar, coconut, pecans, remaining sugar, and

cinnamon. Roll up jellyroll fashion, beginning at short side; moisten edges and seal. Place rolls, seam side down, on greased baking sheets.

Bake at 300° for 55 minutes or until golden brown. Remove to a wire rack, and drizzle with Cinnamon Glaze. Slice and serve warm. Yield: 4 rolls.

Cinnamon Glaze:

2 cups sifted powdered sugar
¼ cup milk
½ teaspoon cinnamon

Combine all ingredients in a small mixing bowl. Beat until smooth. Yield: about 1 cup.

SWEDISH TEA RING

½ cups milk
¼ cups plus 2 tablespoons
 butter or margarine, divided
½ cups sugar, divided
2 packages dry yeast
½ teaspoons salt
7 cups all-purpose flour,
 divided
3 eggs
½ teaspoon vanilla extract
1 tablespoon ground
 cinnamon
½ cups raisins, divided
½ cups chopped pecans,
 divided
2 cups sifted powdered sugar
¼ cup milk

Heat 1½ cups milk and 1 cup butter to 120° to 130° in a medium saucepan; set aside.

Combine ½ cup sugar, yeast, salt, and 2 cups flour in a large mixing bowl. Gradually add warm milk mixture, beating at medium speed of an electric mixer 2 minutes. Add eggs, vanilla, and 2½ cups flour; beat 2 minutes. Gradually add remaining flour to make a soft dough (dough should remain soft and slightly sticky).

Turn dough out onto a lightly floured surface; knead 5 minutes or until smooth and elastic. Cover; let rest 10 minutes.

Shape dough into a ball; place in a well-greased bowl, turning to grease top. Cover and let rise in a warm place (85°), free from drafts, 1½ hours or until doubled in bulk.

Punch dough down; turn out onto a lightly floured surface. Divide into three equal portions, and set aside 2 portions. Roll one portion dough into a 21- x 7-inch rectangle on a lightly floured surface. Melt 2 tablespoons butter, and brush evenly over dough, leaving a 1-inch margin. Combine remaining sugar and cinnamon, stirring well to blend; sprinkle ⅓ cup sugar mixture over dough. Sprinkle ½ cup raisins and ½ cup pecans evenly over dough, leaving a 1-inch margin.

Roll up dough jellyroll fashion, beginning at long side; pinch edges to seal. Place roll on a large, greased baking sheet, seam side down; shape into a ring, and pinch ends together to seal. Repeat procedure with each dough portion.

Make cuts in dough with kitchen shears at 1-inch intervals around ring, cutting two-thirds of the way through roll with each cut. Gently turn each piece of dough on its side, slightly overlapping slices. Repeat procedure for each dough portion.

Cover and let rings rise in a warm place (85°), free from drafts, 30 minutes or until doubled in bulk. Bake at 375° for 20 minutes or until golden brown. Transfer to a wire rack.

Combine powdered sugar and ¼ cup milk; drizzle over rings. Slice and serve warm. Yield: 3 tea rings.

Note: Tea rings freeze well; thaw and heat quickly.

Trade card for Preston and Merrill's Yeast Powder, c.1890.

Collection of Kit Barry, Brattleboro, Vermont

CINNAMON ROLLS

2 packages dry yeast
½ cup lukewarm water (105°
  to 115°)
1½ cups sugar, divided
½ cup milk, scalded
½ cup shortening
2 teaspoons salt
2 eggs, lightly beaten
4½ to 5 cups all-purpose
  flour, divided
½ cup butter or margarine,
  melted
1 tablespoon ground
  cinnamon
1½ cups sifted powdered
  sugar
3 tablespoons milk
1 teaspoon vanilla extract
½ cup chopped pecans,
  toasted

Combine yeast, lukewarm water, and 1 tablespoon sugar in a small mixing bowl; stir well. Let stand 5 minutes.

Combine ¼ cup plus 3 tablespoons sugar, ½ cup scalded milk, shortening, and salt in a large mixing bowl; cool to lukewarm (105° to 115°). Add eggs and 2 cups flour; stir until well blended. Stir in yeast mixture; add enough remaining flour to make a soft dough. Cover and let dough rest 10 minutes.

Turn dough out onto a floured surface, and knead 10 minutes. Shape dough into a ball; place in a lightly greased bowl, turning to grease top. Cover and let rise in a warm place (85°), free from drafts, 1½ hours or until doubled in bulk.

Punch dough down; let rest 10 minutes. Turn dough out onto a lightly floured surface; divide dough into 4 equal portions. Roll each portion into a 12- x 6-inch rectangle; brush with butter, leaving a 1-inch margin on all sides.

Combine remaining 1 cup sugar and cinnamon; sprinkle over each rectangle of dough. Roll up jellyroll fashion, beginning at long side; moisten edges with water to seal.

Cut rolls into 1-inch-thick slices; place slices, cut side down, in four 8-inch round cakepans. Cover and repeat rising

procedure 45 minutes or until doubled in bulk.

Bake at 350° for 20 minutes or until lightly browned. Combine powdered sugar, 3 tablespoons milk, vanilla, and pecans in a small bowl; mix well. Drizzle over warm rolls, and serve. Yield: about 4 dozen.

RED PLUM JAM

8 cups coarsely chopped red
  plums
1 (1¾-ounce) package
  powdered fruit pectin
8 cups sugar

Combine plum pulp and fruit pectin in a Dutch oven. Bring to a boil; cook 1 minute. Stir in sugar; return to a boil. Reduce heat; cook 30 minutes, stirring frequently, or until jam thickens and reaches desired consistency. Skim off foam with a metal spoon; discard.

Ladle jam into hot, sterilized jars, leaving ¼-inch headspace; cover at once with metal lids, and screw bands tight. Process in a boiling-water bath 10 minutes. Yield: 4½ pints.

APPLE BUTTER

8 pounds cooking apples,
  peeled and cored
1 (1¾-ounce) package
  powdered fruit pectin
8 cups sugar
2 teaspoons ground
  cinnamon

Combine apples and water to cover in a large stockpot. Bring to a boil. Reduce heat; cover and cook 15 minutes or until apples are tender. Drain. Press apples through a sieve.

Combine apple pulp and fruit pectin in a large stockpot. Bring to a boil; cook 1 minute. Stir in sugar and cinnamon. Reduce heat; simmer, uncovered, stirring occasionally, 1 hour or until thickened.

Spoon apple jam immediately into hot, sterilized jars, leaving ¼-inch headspace; cover at once with metal lids, and screw bands tight. Process in a boiling-water bath 10 minutes. Yield: 6 pints.

BRUNCH AT MAGNOLIA HALL

Even in a city known for its treasury of antebellum homes, Magnolia Hall of Natchez is truly a crown jewel. One of three outstanding examples of Greek Revival architecture, the mansion was built in 1858 by Thomas Henderson, a merchant-planter. Among the most popular stops on the Natchez Garden Club's annual tour, Magnolia Hall is often the setting for graceful candlelight dinners, luncheons, and brunches served by members of the Garden Club. The last great mansion completed before the outbreak of the Civil War, Magnolia Hall was damaged by fire from the Union gunboat, *Essex*. All damage repaired, original brownstone exterior restored, the lovely home is as hospitable now as when the Hendersons lived there.

ORANGE BLUSH
HAM AND EGGS ALEXANDRIA
SOUTHERN CHEESE GRITS
BRAN MUFFINS
ASSORTED JAMS

Serves 12

Magnolia Hall, Natchez, an architectural jewel on the Garden Club Pilgrimage.

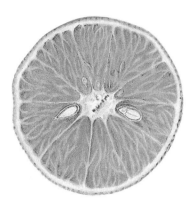

ORANGE BLUSH

2 (6-ounce) cans frozen
  orange juice concentrate,
  thawed and undiluted
2 cups cranberry juice
  cocktail
½ cup sugar
1 (28-ounce) club soda,
  chilled
Crushed ice

Combine orange juice concentrate, cranberry juice cocktail, and sugar in a serving pitcher; stir well to dissolve sugar. Chill thoroughly.

Stir in chilled club soda just before serving. Pour over crushed ice in glasses, and serve. Yield: 12 servings.

HAM AND EGGS ALEXANDRIA

½ pound fresh mushrooms,
  sliced
¼ cup plus 2 tablespoons
  butter or margarine, divided
2 (14-ounce) cans artichoke
  hearts, drained and coarsely
  chopped
3 tablespoons all-purpose
  flour
2 cups milk
1 cup (4 ounces) grated Swiss
  cheese
Salt and pepper to taste
6 English muffins, halved and
  toasted
12 slices baked ham
2 hard-cooked eggs, sliced
1 hard-cooked egg, grated
Pimiento strips

Sauté mushrooms in 2 tablespoons butter in a medium skillet 3 minutes; add artichokes, and sauté an additional 3 minutes. Transfer mushrooms and artichokes to a small bowl.

Melt remaining butter in skillet; add flour, stirring until smooth. Gradually add milk; cook over medium heat, stirring constantly, until thickened. Add cheese, stirring until cheese melts. Stir in mushrooms and artichokes. Add salt and pepper; mix well. Set aside; keep warm.

Arrange toasted muffin halves on a serving platter; place 1 ham slice on each muffin half. Spoon sauce over each ham slice. Garnish each serving with egg slices, grated egg, and pimiento strips. Serve warm. Yield: 12 servings.

SOUTHERN CHEESE GRITS

5 cups water
1½ teaspoons salt
1½ cups uncooked quick grit
1 (6-ounce) roll sharp cheese
  spread
1 (6-ounce) roll garlic-cheese
  spread
¾ cup butter or margarine
4 eggs, beaten
½ cup milk
¼ teaspoon pepper

Bring water and salt to a boil in a large Dutch oven; gradually add grits, stirring constantly. Reduce heat; cook, uncovered, 3 minutes. Add cheese and butter; stir until melted. Add eggs, milk, and pepper; stir well.

Pour mixture into a greased 3-quart casserole. Bake at 350° for 1 hour. Serve immediately. Yield: 12 servings.

BRAN MUFFINS

¾ cup milk
1 cup shreds of wheat bran
  cereal
1 cup all-purpose flour
3 tablespoons sugar
1 tablespoon plus ½ teaspoon
  baking powder
¼ teaspoon salt
1 egg, beaten
3 tablespoons butter or
  margarine, melted

Pour milk over cereal in a small mixing bowl; stir to blend. Let stand 5 minutes.

Sift together flour, sugar, baking powder, and salt in a medium mixing bowl.

Make a well in center of flour mixture. Add cereal, egg, and butter; stir just until dry ingredients are moistened.

Spoon batter into greased muffin pans, filling two-thirds full. Bake at 425° for 25 minutes. Remove from pans immediately. Yield: 1 dozen.

*Brunch at Magnolia Hall
starts with Orange Blush,
followed by Ham and Eggs
Alexandria, Cheese Grits,
and Bran Muffins.*

Buyers turned out when John H. Shary's Southwestern Land Co. offered land in 1930.

SHARY ESTATE BRUNCH

People who winter in the lush, semi-tropical environs of Mission, Texas, will tell you that nowhere in this country may one enjoy more days of the year out in the open. It was this sunny climate that drew John H. Shary, the Nebraska-born land developer to this part of the Rio Grande Valley. He was a visionary who saw beyond the arid brushland; he bought up 36,000 acres in 1914-17, subdivided it into 12-acre tracts, irrigated, and, in 1915, planted the first 300 acres in young citrus trees. This was the beginning of the first large-scale commercial citrus industry in the Valley, which earned for him the title, "Father of the Citrus Industry." Marialice Shary Shivers, wife of Allan Shivers, Jr., former Texas governor, remembers the days of her parents' open-handed hospitality at Sharyland Estate, when this brunch was served.

BROILED GRAPEFRUIT
BROILED QUAIL ON TOAST
BAKED GRITS
ORANGE BISCUITS
STARLIGHT MARMALADE

Serves 6

Collection of Mr. and Mrs. Allan Shivers

BROILED GRAPEFRUIT

3 large grapefruit, halved
¼ cup plus 2 tablespoons
  firmly packed brown sugar
1 tablespoon ground
  cinnamon
¼ teaspoon ground mace
3 tablespoons butter or
  margarine
3 maraschino cherries,
  halved

Section grapefruit and re-move seeds. Set aside.

Combine sugar, cinnamon, and mace; mix well. Sprinkle sugar mixture over grapefruit halves; dot with butter.

Broil grapefruit 4 inches from heat 10 minutes or until lightly browned. Transfer to individual serving dishes; garnish with cherries. Serve warm. Yield: 6 servings.

BROILED QUAIL ON TOAST

12 quail, cleaned and
  flattened
1 tablespoon vegetable oil
12 slices bacon, halved
Salt and pepper to taste
12 slices white bread,
  toasted
6 slices bacon, cooked
  (optional)

Place quail, breast side up, on a greased rack in a roasting pan. Brush each quail lightly with oil. Lay bacon over quail to cover all exposed areas.

Broil quail 6 inches from heat 15 minutes. Remove bacon, and discard. Broil until quail is lightly browned, turning once. Season with salt and pepper. Place quail on toast slices; gar-nish with bacon, if desired. Yield: 6 servings.

John H. Shary was a true developer. In the early 1900s he wooed thousands of newcomers south by sponsoring excur-sion trains to Sharyland; berth and meals cost only $2.00 a day. Many visitors stayed, purchasing small groves, while others invested in the valley, contracting with Shary to manage their property and the produce. In 1925, Shary organized the Rio Grande Valley Citrus As-sociation and by 1933, the valley had over 8 million trees, producing the still-popular Ruby Red and Star Ruby grapefruits.

BAKED GRITS

1 cup uncooked regular grits
2 cups water
2 cups milk
3 tablespoons sugar
1 teaspoon salt
2 eggs, separated
½ cup whipping cream

Combine grits, water, and milk in a medium saucepan; mix well. Bring to a boil; stir in sugar and salt. Reduce heat to medium; continue to cook, uncovered, until mixture thickens and liquid is absorbed. Let cool.

Beat egg yolks lightly; stir into cooled grits mixture. Add whipping cream; mix well.

Beat egg whites (at room temperature) until stiff peaks form. Gently fold into grits mixture. Spoon into a lightly greased 1½-quart casserole. Bake at 350° for 50 minutes. Let stand 10 minutes before serving. Yield: 8 servings.

ORANGE BISCUITS

3 cups all-purpose flour
¼ cup sugar
1 tablespoon baking powder
1 teaspoon salt
½ cup shortening
1 tablespoon grated orange rind
½ teaspoon baking soda
1¼ cups buttermilk
Melted butter or margarine

Combine flour, sugar, baking powder, and salt in a medium mixing bowl. Cut in shortening with a pastry blender until mixture resembles coarse meal. Stir in orange rind.

Dissolve soda in buttermilk; stir well. Pour buttermilk mixture evenly over flour mixture, stirring until dry ingredients are moistened. Turn dough out onto a lightly floured surface; knead 4 to 5 times.

Roll dough to ½-inch thickness; cut with a 2-inch biscuit cutter. Place biscuits on a greased baking sheet; brush with melted butter. Bake at 450° for 10 minutes or until lightly browned. Yield: 1½ dozen.

Gold Medal Flour ad in Ladies' Home Journal, *July, 1904.*

STARLIGHT MARMALADE

1 large grapefruit
½ cup thinly sliced orange rind
4½ quarts water, divided
¾ cup chopped orange sections
1 small lemon, thinly sliced
Sugar

Remove rind from grapefruit; set aside. Chop pulp, and discard seeds. Set pulp aside.

Cut reserved rind into small star-shaped pieces using an aspic cutter; reserve remaining rind pieces. Combine grapefruit rind stars, reserved rind pieces, orange rind, and 1½ quarts water in a large Dutch oven; bring mixture to a boil. Boil, uncovered, 5 minutes; drain. Repeat procedure.

Combine remaining 1½ quarts water, rind, chopped orange, and lemon slices in Dutch oven; bring to a boil, and boil 5 minutes. Cover and let stand 12 to 18 hours in a cool place.

Uncover; bring to a boil. Reduce heat; cook 35 minutes or until rind is tender. Measure amount of fruit and liquid mixture. Add 1 cup sugar per 1 cup mixture; stir well. Bring to a boil; cook, stirring frequently, until mixture registers 220° on candy thermometer.

Pour marmalade into hot sterilized jars, leaving ¼-inch headspace; cover at once with metal lids, and screw bands tight. Process in a boiling-water bath 10 minutes. Yield: about 7 half-pints.

ch menu served at Shary Estate.

SECOND BREAKFAST AT MME. BÉGUÉ'S

In the fall of 1906, Elizabeth Kettenring Dutrey Bégué put down the pots and pans that made her name a household word in New Orleans and was laid to rest. The German woman who married Hypolite Bégué and made their restaurant synonymous with "second breakfast" had become a legend, dating from 1884, when tourists discovered her during the Cotton Centennial Exposition. The gargantuan meal began at eleven and lasted for hours; each guest had his own bottle of wine to beguile the time between countless courses of fish, meat, an egg dish, vegetables—always concluding with fruit and coffee. Madame never joined in; she presided.

BOILED CRAYFISH
FRENCH BREAD
WINE
BROILED SIRLOIN STEAK
OPEN-FACE VEAL OMELET
BAKED STUFFED TOMATOES
FRIED BOILED POTATOES
APPLE WEDGES
ROQUEFORT AND SWISS CHEESES
CAFÉ NOIR

Serves 4

Each guest had his own wine bottle at Mme. Bégué's famous 11 o'clock breakfast in New Orleans.

BOILED CRAYFISH

4 pounds whole crayfish
1 gallon water
3 lemons, halved
3 medium onions, quartered
5 stalks celery, halved
4 cloves garlic
1 tablespoon liquid crab boil
½ teaspoon red pepper

Place crayfish in large pan of cold salted water; let stand 15 minutes. Drain and repeat soaking procedure.

Bring 1 gallon water to a boil in a large stockpot. Remove juice from lemons; add juice and lemons to water. Add next 5 ingredients; return to a boil. Add drained crayfish; boil 3 minutes. Remove from heat; let stand in cooking liquid 30 minutes. Drain and serve warm. Yield: 4 servings.

BROILED SIRLOIN STEAK

1 pound sirloin steak,
  ½-inch-thick
¼ teaspoon salt
Dash of pepper
2 tablespoons butter or
  margarine, melted
2 tablespoons chopped fresh
  parsley

Cut steak into 4 serving-size pieces; season with salt and pepper. Broil 4 inches from heating element 3 to 5 minutes on each side or until desired degree of doneness.

Combine butter and parsley; pour over hot steaks, and serve immediately. Yield: 4 servings.

Above right: Guests pose outside Mme. Bégué's Restaurant opposite the French Market, c.1906. A menu (right) of Bégué's memorable breakfasts.

Madame Begue's Breakfast Menus for a Week.

MONDAY
Broiled Ham
Toast Bread Omelet
Potatoes with White Sauce
Jambalaya of Chicken and Ham
Roast Turkey
Mayonaise of Celery and Shrimps
Fruit
Coffee

TUESDAY
Chicken a la Creole
Kidney with Tomato Sauce
Mayonaise of Fish
Veal Omelet
Stuffed Tomatoes
Pineapple with Port Wine
Coffee

WEDNESDAY
Blanquette of Veal
Spaghetti with Shrimps
Liver a la Begue
Ham Omelet
Strawberries with Madeira Wine
Roast Duck
Coffee

THURSDAY
Broiled Beefsteak
Court Bouillon
Sweetbread Omelet
Broiled Sausage
Fried Eggplant
Fruit
Anchovy Salad
Coffee

FRIDAY
Turtle

Open-Face Veal Omelet,
a Bégué specialty.
Add Baked Stuffed Tomatoes
and French bread.

BAKED STUFFED TOMATOES

4 medium tomatoes
½ cup chopped onion
1½ teaspoons lard
1 cup chopped fresh parsley
1 teaspoon salt
½ teaspoon pepper
Fine, dry breadcrumbs

Slice off top of each tomato; scoop out pulp, leaving shells intact. Chop pulp, and set aside. Invert shells on paper towels to drain.

Sauté pulp and onion in lard in a heavy skillet until tender. Remove from heat; stir in parsley, salt, and pepper. Spoon evenly into tomato shells; sprinkle with breadcrumbs.

Place stuffed tomatoes in a 10- x 6- x 2-inch baking dish. Bake at 350° for 30 minutes or until thoroughly heated. Serve hot. Yield: 4 servings.

FRIED BOILED POTATOES

4 medium potatoes
⅔ cup chopped onion
2 slices bacon, diced
1 tablespoon shortening
¼ teaspoon salt
⅛ teaspoon pepper
Paprika

Combine potatoes and water to cover in a medium saucepan. Cover and bring to a boil. Reduce heat; cover and simmer 20 minutes. Drain; cool slightly, and peel. Cut potatoes into ¼-inch-thick slices, and set aside.

Sauté onion and bacon in a large skillet just until bacon is limp. Add potatoes, shortening, salt, and pepper; cook over medium heat until potatoes are browned, turning frequently.

Remove from heat, and transfer to a warm serving platter. Sprinkle with paprika, and serve hot. Yield: 4 servings.

OPEN-FACE VEAL OMELET

½ pound veal cutlets, chopped
1 cup chopped fresh mushrooms
1 tablespoon grated onion
2 tablespoons shortening, divided
1 tablespoon all-purpose flour
6 eggs
¼ cup milk
1 tablespoon chopped fresh parsley
½ teaspoon salt
⅛ teaspoon pepper
Paprika (optional)
3 fresh mushrooms, sliced
1 tablespoon butter or margarine

Sauté veal, mushrooms, and onion in 1 tablespoon shortening in a large skillet until veal is no longer pink and vegetables are tender. Stir in flour.

Combine eggs, milk, parsley, salt, and pepper in a medium mixing bowl; beat well. Stir in veal mixture.

Melt remaining shortening in a 10-inch skillet. Pour egg mixture into skillet. Cover and cook over low heat 25 minutes or until set. Sprinkle with paprika, if desired.

Sauté sliced mushrooms in butter until tender. Arrange over omelet. Cut omelet into wedges, and serve immediately. Yield: 4 servings.

GALVESTON WINTER BILL OF FARE

To build Galveston's Beach Hotel in 1883, architect Nicholas J. Clayton revived the then-unfashionable mansard roof style. He combined it with curved and pointed Gothic arches and delicate wooden "stick" construction and set it on 300 deep piles at the water's edge. For color, there was no building to compare; the roof was painted in Siennese red and white stripes. The three-story building, its ornate grillwork and gables were mauve and golden green. The crowning dome rose 125 feet from the ground. "Migratory birds of fashion" swarmed; President Benjamin Harrison tarried there. Chefs, from a separate kitchen, served food as exquisite as the setting with seven-course breakfasts as sumptuous as the menu included here.

SARDINES ON TOAST
SWEETBREADS WITH GREEN PEAS
BROILED FILET MIGNON
FRIED OYSTERS
BREAKFAST PUFFS
RAISIN WAFFLES
FRESH ORANGE WEDGES

Serves 6

The Beach Hotel in Galveston, Texas, a mecca for distinguished guests, c.1890.

SARDINES ON TOAST

3 (4.375-ounce) cans
  sardines, undrained
Juice of 3 medium lemons
3 tablespoons Worcestershire
  sauce
⅛ teaspoon hot sauce
6 slices bread, toasted

Drain sardines, reserving liquid. Set sardines aside. Combine sardine liquid, lemon juice, Worcestershire sauce, and hot sauce in a small skillet; bring to a boil. Reduce heat, and add sardines; cook, stirring gently, until thoroughly heated.

Place 3 sardines on each slice of toast; pour pan drippings over sardines. Serve immediately. Yield: 6 servings.

SWEETBREADS WITH GREEN PEAS

1 pound veal sweetbreads
2 quarts water
2 tablespoons vinegar
2¼ teaspoons salt, divided
1 egg, beaten
2 tablespoons water
½ cup fine, dry breadcrumbs
¼ teaspoon pepper
Lard
1 (15½-ounce) can green
  peas, undrained
2 tablespoons butter or
  margarine
Fresh parsley sprigs

Place sweetbreads with water to cover in a medium mixing bowl. Soak for 1 hour. Drain well; remove and discard white membrane.

Combine drained sweetbreads, 2 quarts water, vinegar, and 2 teaspoons salt in a large Dutch oven. Bring mixture to a boil. Reduce heat; cover and simmer 20 minutes.

Remove sweetbreads, and cut into serving-size pieces. Combine egg and 2 tablespoons water in a small bowl; set aside. Combine breadcrumbs, remaining salt, and pepper in a small bowl; set aside. Dip sweetbreads in egg mixture; roll in breadcrumb mixture.

Melt lard in a large skillet over medium heat. Add sweetbreads; cook over low heat 10 minutes or until browned, turning to brown all sides. Remove sweetbreads; drain.

Cook peas in a medium saucepan over medium heat until hot. Drain and add butter.

Serve peas in a small bowl on a platter. Place sweetbreads around bowl on platter; garnish with parsley. Serve immediately. Yield: 6 servings.

Purchaser tries out a new General Electric toaster, c.1905.

BROILED FILET MIGNON

1 (2-pound) beef tenderloin,
  trimmed
6 slices bread, toasted
Salt and pepper to taste
½ cup butter or margarine,
  melted
1 tablespoon chopped fresh
  parsley
Lemon slices (optional)

Cut beef tenderloin into six 1-inch-thick slices.

Place steaks on a well-greased rack in a shallow roasting pan. Broil steaks 6 inches from heating element 10 minutes on each side or until desired degree of doneness.

Place each fillet on a slice of toast. Transfer to a warm serving platter, and sprinkle with salt and pepper. Drizzle with melted butter, and sprinkle with chopped parsley. Garnish platter with lemon slices, if desired. Yield: 6 servings.

Raisin Waffles are a treat when served with cane syrup and a pretty garnish of orange wedges.

FRIED OYSTERS

1 (12-ounce) container Select oysters, drained
¼ teaspoon salt
⅛ teaspoon pepper
1 cup all-purpose flour
2 eggs, lightly beaten
1 cup cracker crumbs
Vegetable oil

Sprinkle oysters with salt and pepper; dredge in flour. Dip oysters in egg; dredge in cracker crumbs. Repeat dipping and dredging procedure to coat well.

Fry oysters in deep hot oil (375°) until golden brown; drain on paper towels. Serve hot. Yield: 6 servings.

BREAKFAST PUFFS

1 egg
½ cup milk
1⅓ cups all-purpose flour
⅓ cup sugar
2½ teaspoons baking powder
¼ teaspoon salt
1 teaspoon shortening, melted
Vegetable oil

Beat egg in a medium mixing bowl until light and frothy; add milk, mixing well. Combine flour, sugar, baking powder, and salt in a small mixing bowl; stir well. Sift dry ingredients together; add to egg mixture, beating well. Stir in melted shortening.

Drop mixture by tablespoonfuls into deep hot oil (375°). Fry until puffs are golden brown, turning once. Drain on paper towels. Serve hot. Yield: 2 dozen.

RAISIN WAFFLES

1 cup chopped raisins
1½ cups all-purpose flour, divided
1 tablespoon baking powder
1 teaspoon salt
1 cup milk
2 eggs, separated
1 tablespoon butter or margarine, melted

Dredge raisins in ¼ cup flour; set aside. Combine remaining flour, baking powder, and salt; mix well. Add milk, egg yolks, and butter; mix until well blended. Stir in raisins.

Beat egg whites (at room temperature) until stiff peaks form; gently fold into raisin mixture.

Spoon batter onto a preheated, lightly oiled waffle iron, following manufacturer's directions. Cook 5 minutes or until golden brown. Remove waffle, and keep warm. Repeat procedure with remaining batter. Serve waffles warm with cane syrup. Yield: six 4-inch waffles.

1904 BREAKFAST AT NOON

The brilliance of Galveston's social life before and after the turn of the century was epitomized by the rich, eccentric family of James Moreau Brown, who built Ashton Villa in 1860. Mathilda Brown Sweeney inherited the villa, but the most colorful member of the clan was Miss Rebecca Ashton Brown. The liberated Rebecca traveled the world, wore what she pleased, every thread of which was written up in the paper, and was held in awe by her townsmen. Ashton Villa was filled with her accumulation of travel mementos, and guests entertained there were assured of material to talk over for weeks. Unlike less secure hostesses, Rebecca Brown did not have to read how-to books on parties and menus; she "wrote the book." Once she did a thing, it was correct. If she'd given this noon breakfast, it would have been worth at least two columns and the writer would have termed it *recherché*.

MORNING PICK-UP
HONEY DEW MELON WITH FRESH BLUEBERRIES
POACHED REDFISH
FRESH FIG MUFFINS
EGGS FLORENTINE
LEMON TEA BISCUITS

Serves 8

MORNING PICK-UP

3 cups milk
¼ cup port wine
¼ cup light rum
1 tablespoon sugar
Crushed ice
Ground nutmeg

Combine milk, wine, rum, and sugar, mixing well. Chill. Pour over crushed ice in tall glasses. Sprinkle with ground nutmeg, and serve immediately. Yield: 8 servings.

POACHED REDFISH

1½ quarts water
½ large lemon
1 onion, sliced
1 stalk celery, quartered
1 sprig fresh thyme
1 bay leaf
3 tablespoons salt
1 tablespoon vinegar
1 teaspoon Worcestershire sauce
½ teaspoon hot sauce
1 (5-pound) whole-dressed redfish, fins and eyes removed

Place a rack in the bottom of a large shallow roasting pan or fish poacher. Add 1½ quarts water and next 9 ingredients. Place pan over 2 surface units on stovetop; bring mixture to a boil. Reduce heat; cover and simmer 30 minutes.

Add redfish; cover and cook over medium heat 10 minutes per inch of thickness of fish. Remove fish to a warm serving platter. Serve immediately or refrigerate, and serve chilled. Yield: 8 servings.

FRESH FIG MUFFINS

2 large fresh figs, finely chopped
2 cups plus 2 tablespoons all-purpose flour, divided
⅓ cup sugar
1 tablespoon baking powder
½ teaspoon salt
1 cup milk
1 egg, beaten
¼ cup butter or margarine, melted

Dredge figs in 2 tablespoons flour, tossing lightly to coat well; set aside.

Combine remaining flour, sugar, baking powder, and salt in a medium mixing bowl; sift together 4 times. Stir together milk, egg, and butter; add to dry ingredients, stirring until dry ingredients are moistened. Fold in reserved figs.

Spoon batter into greased muffin pans, filling two-thirds full. Bake at 450° for 20 minutes or until golden brown. Remove from pans, and serve immediately. Yield: about 1 dozen.

Morning Pick-Up is an update of traditional milk punch. Eggs Florentine and Fresh Fig Muffins: sure to please.

LEMON TEA BISCUITS

2 cups all-purpose flour
¼ cup plus 2 tablespoons sugar, divided
1 tablespoon plus 1 teaspoon baking powder
½ teaspoon baking soda
½ teaspoon salt
1 tablespoon plus 1½ teaspoons grated lemon rind, divided
¼ cup plus 2 tablespoons shortening
¾ cup buttermilk
¼ teaspoon lemon extract
¼ teaspoon lemon juice

Sift together flour, 2 tablespoons sugar, baking powder, soda, and salt in a medium mixing bowl. Stir in 1 tablespoon lemon rind. Cut in shortening using a pastry blender until mixture resembles coarse meal. Add buttermilk and lemon extract, stirring until dry ingredients are moistened.

Turn dough out onto a lightly floured surface; knead lightly 10 to 12 times.

Roll dough to ¼-inch thickness; cut with a 1¾-inch biscuit cutter.

Combine remaining sugar, lemon rind, and juice in a small bowl. Sprinkle ¼ teaspoon mixture over half of biscuits. Top with remaining biscuits, pressing together lightly.

Place biscuits on greased baking sheets. Bake at 450° for 8 minutes or until golden brown. Remove from baking sheet, and serve immediately. Yield: about 2 dozen.

EGGS FLORENTINE

4 pounds fresh spinach
8 eggs
Salt to taste
1 (13-ounce) can evaporated milk
8 ounces process American cheese
2 cups buttered soft breadcrumbs
4 cups cooked, mashed potatoes

Remove stems from spinach; wash leaves thoroughly in lukewarm water. Place in a Dutch oven (do not add water). Cook over high heat 3 to 5 minutes. Drain spinach well; chop.

Divide spinach evenly into eight 10-ounce custard cups. Carefully break 1 egg on top of spinach in each cup. Sprinkle each with salt; set aside.

Combine milk and cheese in top of a double boiler. Cook over boiling water, stirring occasionally, until cheese melts. Pour cheese sauce over eggs; top with buttered breadcrumbs.

Place custard cups in two 13- x 9- x 2-inch baking pans, and pour hot water into pans to a depth of ½ inch. Bake at 350° for 25 minutes.

Place custard cups on a baking sheet. Pipe mashed potatoes around edges of custard cups. Broil 6 inches from heating element 2 minutes or until potatoes are browned. Serve immediately. Yield: 8 servings.

INVITATION TO BRUNCH

Brunch as a ploy for entertaining can do justice to any event; we use it to open or close an important season or to fête a guest of honor. Or the brunch itself can be a happening, breathing life into an otherwise so-so weekend.

The breakfast we know as brunch has been used inventively since before the turn of the century. In the late 1800s, a group of Atlanta businessmen had a dime-limit poker club they called the Icepicks. Every Saturday night they played, closing at midnight with a breakfast of champagne, Smithfield ham, and game birds. In the early 1900s, Atlanta turned out a fine breakfast on the occasion of the Metropolitan Opera's first appearance in the city, delighting many of the company with their first taste of cheese grits.

Our major holidays offer abundant opportunities for brunching. Our Thanksgiving party menu thoughtfully omits turkey, on the theory that guests will have their fill of the traditional bird at dinner later in the day.

Sporting events offer irresistible challenges to our brunchmanship. Alumni and other interested parties get together over aperitifs and conjure up the old team spirit with plenty of strengthening food. A group of University of Kentucky fans living in Louisville regularly charter a bus to attend U.K.'s home games in Lexington. During the hour-plus ride, a hearty champagne brunch enlivens the miles, producing about forty rooters ready to cheer their team to a victorious finish.

A law unto itself is the Hunt Breakfast. To Southerners who follow the old English sport of riding to hounds, any meal pertaining to the hunt is a breakfast. In some hunts, members may prepare the food in advance; others employ caterers. The locale may be the home of the Master of Hounds, as is the case with the Mells Hunt in Waco, Tennessee, or the clubhouse. But good food is always a traditional part of the hunt festivities.

Weddings afford another approach to brunches; no better way exists for entertaining the out-of-towners before an afternoon bridal affair. We nearly always serve eggs at brunch, for, as Marion Harland said, "They are nutritious, popular, and never . . . an unelegant or homely dish."

MENU OF MENUS

THANKSGIVING
BREAKFAST

MOORELAND HUNT
BREAKFAST

BEFORE THE GAME

BEFORE THE WEDDING

CANASTA CLUB BRUNCH

NEW YEAR'S EVE
MIDNIGHT BRUNCH

A Thanksgiving Breakfast at the Hammond-Harwood House features Baked Ham, (clockwise) Fresh Broccoli Salad, Tomato Pie, Sally Lunn, Buttery Fried Oysters, and Beaten Biscuits.

THANKSGIVING BREAKFAST

In planning a Thanksgiving breakfast of this scope, we assume a turkey dinner later, prepared by someone else, somewhere else! Old Maryland Baked Ham is no problem; it cools overnight and is ready to be finished in the oven in time for breakfast. There is historical precedent here, even for the salad: Broccoli lightly cooked and served as a salad goes back to 1798. Toddy, of course! Colonials made toddies and juleps with Jamaican rum, brandy, or hard cider for a century before that deathless Scotch-Irish contribution to civilization: corn whiskey made from corn.

HOT APPLE TODDY
BUTTERY FRIED OYSTERS
OLD MARYLAND BAKED HAM
FRESH BROCCOLI SALAD IN LETTUCE CUPS
TOMATO PIE
BEATEN BISCUITS
SALLY LUNN
BAKED GINGER APPLES
MARYLAND ROCKS

Serves 10 to 12

Thanksgiving Day/Ways and Means, *from* Harper's Weekly, *1858.*

HOT APPLE TODDY

3 large baking apples
½ cup water
1 quart boiling water
½ cup sugar
2 quarts apple juice
2 quarts Irish whiskey
2 cups Jamaican rum
3 lemon rinds cut in long
  spirals
50 whole cloves
1 (4-inch) stick cinnamon
1½ teaspoons ground
  nutmeg

Core apples; peel top third of each. Place apples in a shallow baking dish; add ½ cup water. Cover and bake at 350° for 45 minutes or until apples are tender, basting occasionally.

Place baked apples in a large stainless steel stockpot. Add 1 quart boiling water and sugar. Simmer, uncovered, 30 minutes, stirring occasionally.

Add apple juice, whiskey, and rum to mixture; stir well, and simmer, uncovered, 1 hour.

Stir in lemon rind, cloves, cinnamon, and nutmeg; simmer, uncovered, an additional hour. Remove whole spices, and discard. Serve hot in warm serving cups. Yield: about 1 gallon.

A Thanksgiving postcard, c.1920.

BUTTERY FRIED OYSTERS

2 (12-ounce) containers
  Select oysters, drained
½ teaspoon salt
¼ teaspoon pepper
3 eggs, lightly beaten
3 cups soft breadcrumbs
½ cup butter

Rinse oysters thoroughly in cold water; pat dry, and sprinkle with salt and pepper. Dip oysters in egg, and dredge in breadcrumbs. Repeat dipping and dredging procedure to coat oysters well.

Melt butter in a skillet over medium heat; add oysters and cook until golden brown, turning once. Drain well on paper towels. Serve hot. Yield: 10 to 12 appetizer servings.

OLD MARYLAND BAKED HAM

1 (13-pound) country ham
1 cup vinegar
25 whole cloves
⅔ cup firmly packed brown
  sugar
3 tablespoons sherry

Place ham in a very large container; cover with cold water. Soak ham overnight. Pour off water, and scrub ham thoroughly with a stiff brush. Rinse.

Place ham in a large stockpot; cover with water, and add vinegar. Bring to a boil; reduce heat. Cover and simmer 3½ hours.

Remove from heat; cool ham in cooking liquid. Remove ham from cooking liquid, reserving 2 cups; discard remaining cooking liquid.

Remove tough outer skin from ham, and discard. Place ham, fat side up, in a shallow roasting pan. Score fat in a diamond pattern. Add reserved cooking liquid. Bake at 350° for 1 hour or until browned.

Remove from oven. Place whole cloves in points of diamond pattern. Combine brown sugar and sherry in a small mixing bowl; spoon over ham. Return to oven for 15 minutes or until glazed. Cool completely.

Transfer ham to a serving platter. Cut into thin slices to serve. Yield: 10 to 12 servings.

Note: Remaining ham may be covered and stored in refrigerator for later use.

Thanksgiving getaway features turkeys in a "cornmobile."

FRESH BROCCOLI SALAD IN LETTUCE CUPS

3 pounds fresh broccoli
1 cup vegetable oil
½ cup cider vinegar
2 teaspoons prepared mustard
1 teaspoon salt
Red pepper rings
Lettuce leaves
Grated hard-cooked egg yolk

Wash broccoli thoroughly; cut into flowerettes, discarding tough ends and lower stalks. Arrange broccoli in a steaming rack. Place over boiling water; cover and steam 10 minutes or to desired degree of doneness. Plunge immediately into ice water. Drain thoroughly. Transfer broccoli to a serving dish; cover and chill.

Combine oil, vinegar, mustard, and salt in a small jar; shake vigorously. Spoon dressing over broccoli; toss lightly.

Place red pepper rings on lettuce leaves, and spoon broccoli into rings. Garnish with grated egg yolk, and serve immediately. Yield: 10 to 12 servings.

TOMATO PIE

6 medium-size ripe tomatoes, peeled, cored, and halved crosswise
1 teaspoon salt, divided
¼ teaspoon pepper, divided
3 tablespoons firmly packed brown sugar, divided
3 cups soft breadcrumbs, divided
3 tablespoons butter or margarine, divided

Place 6 tomato halves in a greased 10-inch deep-dish pie-plate. Sprinkle evenly with half of salt, pepper, and brown sugar. Top with 1½ cups breadcrumbs; dot with half the butter. Repeat layers with remaining ingredients.

Bake at 350° for 30 minutes or until golden brown. Cut into wedges to serve. Yield: 10 to 12 servings.

BEATEN BISCUITS

7 cups all-purpose flour
½ teaspoon baking powder
1½ teaspoons sugar
1½ teaspoons salt
¾ cup lard
2½ cups ice water

Combine flour, baking powder, sugar, and salt in a large mixing bowl, stirring well. Cut in lard with a pastry blender until the mixture resembles coarse meal. Sprinkle 2½ cups ice water evenly over flour mixture, stirring until dry ingredients are moistened.

Turn dough out onto a lightly floured surface. Beat dough with a rolling pin or mallet for 30 minutes or until blisters appear, folding dough over frequently.

Shape dough into 1-inch balls; flatten balls and prick with the tines of a fork. Place biscuits on ungreased baking sheets. Bake at 500° for 20 minutes or until biscuits are lightly browned. Yield: about 3 dozen.

SALLY LUNN

1 package dry yeast
½ cup lukewarm water (105°
   to 115°)
1 cup lukewarm milk (105°
   to 115°)
½ cup butter or margarine,
   melted
¼ cup sugar
2 teaspoons salt
3 eggs, well beaten
5½ cups all-purpose flour,
   divided

Dissolve yeast in lukewarm water in a large mixing bowl. Let stand 5 minutes or until bubbly. Stir in milk, butter, sugar, salt, eggs, and 3 cups flour. Beat at medium speed of an electric mixer 1 minute or until well blended. Stir in remaining flour to make a soft dough. Cover and let rise in a warm place (85°), free from drafts, 1 hour or until doubled in bulk.

Stir dough down; spoon into a well-greased and floured 10-inch Bundt pan. Cover and repeat rising procedure 45 minutes or until doubled in bulk. Bake at 400° for 25 minutes or until bread sounds hollow when tapped. Let cool 10 minutes in pan. Remove from pan; place on a wire rack to cool. Serve warm or cold. Yield: 10 to 12 servings.

Note: Cold bread may be sliced, buttered, and toasted, if desired.

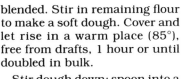

BAKED GINGER APPLES

12 baking apples, washed and
   cored
1 (2.7-ounce) jar crystallized
   ginger, chopped
⅔ cup firmly packed brown
   sugar
1 cup whipping cream

Place apples in a 13- x 9- x 2-inch baking pan. Combine ginger and sugar in a small mixing bowl. Fill each apple core with mixture. Add water to pan to a depth of ½ inch.

Bake at 350° for 45 minutes or until apples are tender. Let cool in pan. Transfer apples to individual serving bowls using a slotted spoon. Pour whipping cream over top. Serve immediately. Yield: 10 to 12 servings.

MARYLAND ROCKS

1 cup butter or margarine,
   softened
1½ cups firmly packed
   brown sugar
3 eggs
2½ cups all-purpose flour
1 teaspoon baking soda
1 teaspoon ground cinnamon
1 (15-ounce) package raisins
2 cups chopped walnuts

Cream 1 cup butter in a large mixing bowl; gradually add brown sugar, beating well. Add eggs, one at a time, beating well after each addition.

Combine flour, soda, and cinnamon in a medium mixing bowl; stir well. Dredge raisins and walnuts in ¼ cup flour mixture in a small mixing bowl. Add remaining flour mixture to creamed mixture, stirring well. Stir in dredged raisin mixture.

Drop dough by teaspoonfuls, 1½ inches apart, onto greased baking sheets. Bake at 350° for 10 minutes or until golden brown. Cool slighty on baking sheets before removing to wire racks. Yield: 9 dozen.

Baked Ginger Apples with Maryland Rocks for munching.

MOORELAND HUNT BREAKFAST

"Tally-Ho!" The cry goes up when a fox is sighted during one of the many hunts that occur every fall in the South as it has done since 1650, when Robert Brook came to Maryland from England, bringing his hunting dogs with him. Following the old English sport of riding to hounds, riders have polished their tack to high gloss, and brushed and braided their mounts. After a bracing stirrup cup, the hunters mount up, their breath visible in the chilly air. The hounds are manic with anxiety to be off. With advance permission from farmers over whose lands they'll ride, the hunt makes a noisy start. No longer a blood sport, fox hunting is an exuberant exercise for man, horse, and dog. The appetites generated by the outdoor gambol are enormous, tailor-made to enjoy this menu served after the Mooreland Hunt in north Alabama.

PASSION PUNCH
FRESH PINEAPPLE AND STRAWBERRIES
CHICKEN À LA KING
CHEESE GRITS SOUFFLÉ
RIVERBOAT SALAD
ANGEL BISCUITS
MINIATURE SWEET ROLLS
CONGO BARS
BROWNIE SQUARES

Serves 8

A Nathaniel Currier lithograph entitled Fox Chase/Gone Away, *dated 1846.*

Passion Punch packs a wallop; brandy and Cointreau do wonders for apple cider!

PASSION PUNCH

4 cups apple cider
2½ cups apple brandy
½ cup cherry brandy
2 teaspoons Cointreau

Combine all ingredients; stir well. Chill. Pour into a punch bowl and serve over crushed ice. Yield: about 7 cups.

The South's oldest sporting tradition is the fox hunt. It dates back to 1650, when Robert Brooke came to Maryland from England, bringing his hunting dogs with him. Interestingly, thoroughbred and stardardbred horses are rarely used in the hunt.

CHICKEN À LA KING

1 cup sliced fresh
  mushrooms
½ cup chopped green pepper
2 tablespoons butter or
  margarine
2 tablespoons all-purpose
  flour
¾ teaspoon salt
2 cups half-and-half
3 cups chopped, cooked
  chicken
2 tablespoons sherry
1 teaspoon lemon juice
1 teaspoon onion juice
3 egg yolks
¼ cup butter or margarine,
  softened
½ teaspoon paprika
¼ cup drained, diced
  pimiento
8 baked commercial patty
  shells

Sauté mushrooms and green pepper in 2 tablespoons butter in a large skillet until tender. Remove vegetables, and set aside. Add flour and salt to pan drippings, stirring until smooth. Cook 1 minute, stirring constantly. Gradually add half-and-half; cook over medium heat, stirring constantly, until thickened and bubbly. Stir in chicken. Reduce heat to low.

Add sherry, lemon juice, and onion juice, mixing well; cook 3 minutes or until bubbly. Combine egg yolks, softened butter, and paprika in a small mixing bowl; beat well. Add yolk mixture to chicken mixture, stirring constantly. Cook 2 to 3 minutes. Stir in pimiento and reserved vegetables.

Spoon chicken mixture into a chafing dish. Spoon evenly into patty shells to serve. Yield: 8 servings.

Chicken à la King, hot in a chafing dish, ready for the patty shells. Riverboat Salad blooms when Century-Old French Dressing goes on.

RIVERBOAT SALAD

1 large bunch leaf lettuce, torn into bite-size pieces
3 radishes, sliced
2 green onions, chopped
1 cup cauliflowerettes
½ cup chopped celery
½ cup scraped, sliced carrots
¼ cup chopped green pepper
2 tomatoes, peeled and chopped
Century-Old French Dressing

Combine first 7 ingredients in a large bowl; toss gently. Add tomatoes just before serving; toss gently. Serve salad with Century-Old French Dressing. Yield: 8 servings.

Century-Old French Dressing:

1 cup water
½ cup sugar
½ cup lemon juice
½ cup vinegar
2 cups olive oil
1 cup catsup
2 teaspoons celery salt
½ teaspoon salt
½ teaspoon white pepper
1 large onion, grated
2 cloves garlic, minced
2½ ounces blue cheese, crumbled

Combine water and sugar in a small saucepan; bring to a boil. Boil 10 minutes. Stir in lemon juice; boil an additional 5 minutes. Remove from heat; let cool. Stir in vinegar. Transfer mixture to a large mixing bowl.

Gradually add oil, beating constantly. Add remaining ingredients; beat until thickened and well blended. Cover; refrigerate. Yield: about 6 cups.

CHEESE GRITS SOUFFLÉ

1 cup uncooked regular grits
1 pound sharp Cheddar cheese, shredded
1 cup whipping cream
1 teaspoon salt
½ teaspoon ground mace
¼ teaspoon red pepper
6 eggs
2 teaspoons baking powder

Cook grits in a large Dutch oven according to package directions. Add cheese; stir until cheese melts. Stir in whipping cream, salt, mace, and pepper; cool completely.

Beat eggs lightly; add baking powder, and beat until well blended. Fold egg mixture into grits mixture. Spoon into a lightly greased 3-quart casserole. Bake at 375° for 50 minutes or until golden brown. Let soufflé stand 10 minutes before serving. Yield: 8 to 10 servings.

ANGEL BISCUITS

1 package dry yeast
½ cup lukewarm water (105°
  to 115°)
5 cups all-purpose flour
1 tablespoon plus 2
  teaspoons baking powder
2½ teaspoons salt
¾ cup shortening
1 teaspoon baking soda
2 cups buttermilk
3 tablespoons sugar

Combine yeast and lukewarm water, stirring to dissolve; let stand 5 minutes or until bubbly. Set aside.

Combine flour, baking powder, and salt in a large bowl; cut in shortening with a pastry blender until mixture resembles coarse meal. Dissolve soda in buttermilk; add to flour mixture, stirring with a fork. Stir in sugar and dissolved yeast; mix well. Cover tightly; refrigerate 8 hours or overnight.

Turn dough out onto a lightly floured surface, and knead 4 to 5 times.

Roll dough to ½-inch thickness; cut with a 2-inch biscuit cutter. Place biscuits in 3 greased 8-inch square baking pans. Cover and let rise 1 hour or until doubled in bulk. Bake at 400° for 12 minutes or until biscuits are lightly browned. Yield: about 4 dozen.

MINIATURE SWEET ROLLS

1 package dry yeast
1 teaspoon sugar
2 cups lukewarm water (105°
  to 115°), divided
6 cups all-purpose flour
½ cup sugar
1 teaspoon salt
¾ cup shortening
1 egg, beaten
2 cups sugar
2 cups chopped pecans
2 tablespoons ground
  cinnamon
¼ cup butter or margarine,
  melted
Glaze (recipe follows)

Combine yeast, 1 teaspoon sugar, and 1 cup lukewarm water in a small bowl; stir well. Let stand 5 minutes.

Combine flour, ½ cup sugar, and salt in a large mixing bowl; stir well. Cut in shortening with a pastry blender until mixture resembles coarse meal. Stir in egg. Add yeast mixture and remaining lukewarm water, beating well. Beat at medium speed of an electric mixer 5 minutes. Cover; refrigerate overnight.

Turn dough out onto a lightly floured surface; divide in half. Roll each half into a 30- x 8-inch rectangle. Combine 2 cups sugar, pecans, cinnamon, and butter; sprinkle over rectangles.

Roll up each rectangle, jellyroll fashion, beginning at long side. Cut rolls into ½-inch slices; place slices, cut side down, in 2 greased 15- x 10- x 1-inch jellyroll pans. Cover and let rise in a warm place (85°), free from drafts, 30 minutes or until doubled in bulk. Bake at 400° for 12 minutes or until lightly browned. Drizzle glaze over tops of warm rolls, and serve immediately. Yield: about 7 dozen.

Glaze:

3 cups sifted powdered sugar
3 to 4 tablespoons milk
¼ teaspoon vanilla extract
Pinch of salt

Combine all ingredients in a saucepan; stir over low heat until smooth. Yield: 1 cup.

Trade card for Best Biscuits and Crackers, c.1900.

BEST BISCUITS AND CRACKERS IN THE UNIVERSE ARE MADE BY RICE & HAYWARD ASK FOR THEM ALWAYS

CONGO BARS

⅔ cup butter or margarine, melted
2⅓ cups firmly packed brown sugar
3 eggs
2¾ cups all-purpose flour
2½ teaspoons baking powder
½ teaspoon salt
1 (6-ounce) package semisweet chocolate morsels
1 cup chopped pecans

Combine butter and sugar in a medium mixing bowl; mix well. Add eggs, flour, baking powder, salt, chocolate, and pecans; mix well.

Spoon mixture into a greased 15- x 10- x 1-inch jellyroll pan. Bake at 350° for 25 to 30 minutes. Cool in pan; cut into 3- x 2-inch bars. Yield: 25 bars.

BROWNIE SQUARES

½ cup butter or margarine
2 (1-ounce) squares semisweet chocolate
1 cup sugar
2 eggs
1 cup all-purpose flour
1 cup chopped pecans
1 teaspoon vanilla extract
Chocolate Frosting (recipe follows)

Melt butter and chocolate in a small saucepan over low heat, stirring constantly. Remove from heat, and cool.

Combine sugar and eggs in a medium mixing bowl; beat with an electric mixer until blended. Add chocolate mixture and flour; beat just until smooth. Stir in pecans and vanilla.

Pour batter into a greased 8-inch square baking pan. Bake at 350° for 20 to 25 minutes. Cool in pan. Spread with Chocolate Frosting; cut into 2-inch squares. Yield: 16 squares.

Chocolate Frosting:

1 cup sifted powdered sugar
2 tablespoons half-and-half
1 tablespoon cocoa
1 tablespoon butter or margarine

Combine all ingredients in a small saucepan; cook over low heat until mixture boils around edge of pan. Remove from heat; beat at medium speed of an electric mixer until desired spreading consistency is reached. Yield: frosting for one 8-inch square pan of brownies.

Trade card for Mack's Milk Chocolate, 1900. Instant chocolate drink is that old!

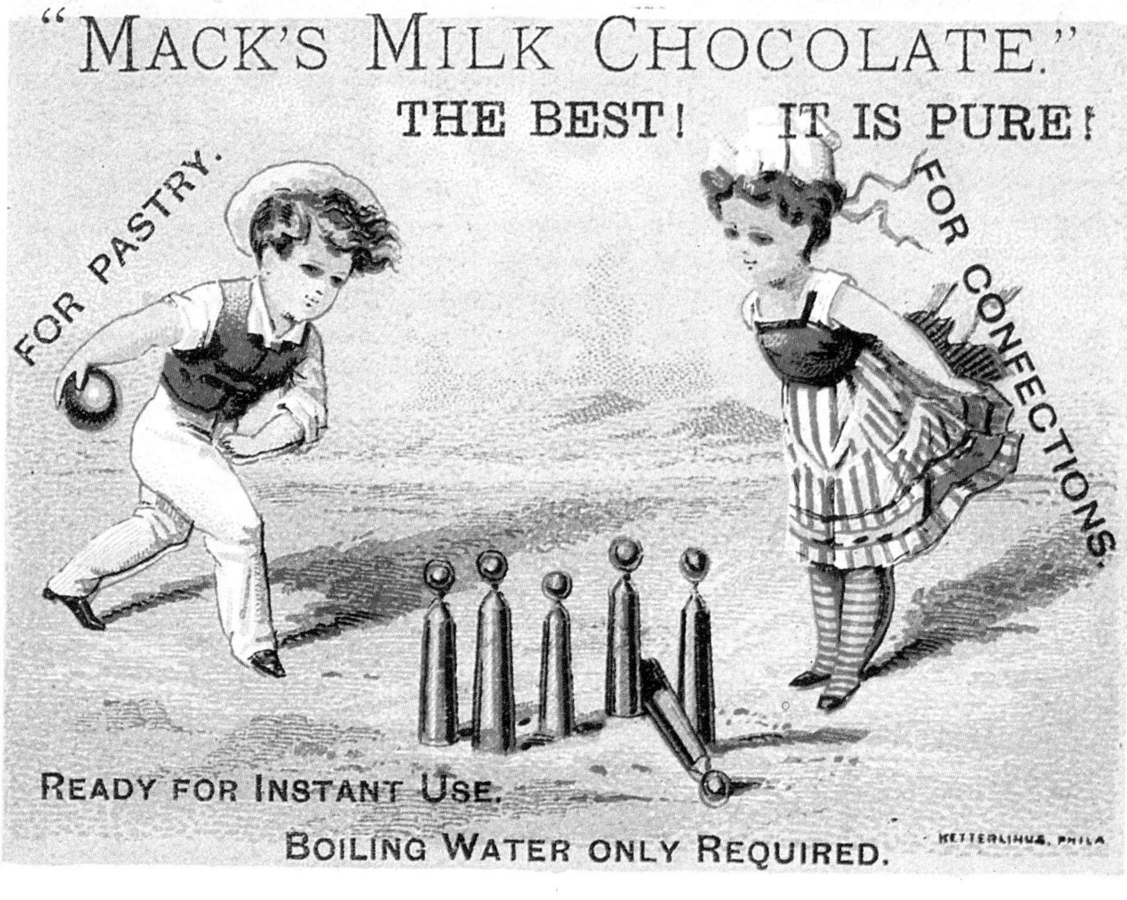

"MACK'S MILK CHOCOLATE."
THE BEST! IT IS PURE!
FOR PASTRY.
FOR CONFECTIONS.
READY FOR INSTANT USE.
BOILING WATER ONLY REQUIRED.
KETTERLINUS, PHILA

This 1918 lunch before a football game foreshadowed the tailgate picnic.

BEFORE THE GAME

Many football fans, as we have noted, have taken the tailgate picnic to their hearts, spreading their pre-game meal in the stadium's shadow, rain or shine. Less hardy souls opt for a hefty brunch at home by way of psyching themselves up for the fray. Georgia, for example, is well populated with avid fans, and many's the brunch that precedes the games played by Tech, Georgia, and the Atlanta Falcons. Daytime parties like this are favored by men as well as women; everyone feels rested, unhurried. A bracing Bloody Sam, so named because, during Prohibition, it was made with gin instead of vodka, leads to the food. Spectators need energy too.

BLOODY SAM
SAUSAGE AND EGG CASSEROLE
FRESH FRUIT SALAD
ICEBOX POTATO ROLLS
ALMOND PUFF COFFEE CAKE

Serves 12

BLOODY SAM

1 (46-ounce) can cocktail
  vegetable juice
2 cups gin
¼ cup lime juice
1 tablespoon Worcestershire
  sauce
1 teaspoon seasoned salt
½ teaspoon hot sauce
Additional seasoned salt
Ice cubes
Celery stalks
Lime wedges

Combine first 6 ingredients in
a large pitcher, mixing well.
Chill thoroughly.

Dip rims of glasses in additional seasoned salt; fill with ice
cubes. Pour tomato mixture
over ice. Garnish with celery
and lime. Yield: 2 quarts.

SAUSAGE AND EGG CASSEROLE

4 slices bread, cubed
1½ pounds bulk pork sausage
9 eggs, beaten
3 cups milk
1½ cups (6 ounces) shredded
  sharp Cheddar cheese
1 teaspoon salt
Tomato rose
Fresh parsley sprigs

Place bread cubes in bottom
of a greased 2½-quart baking
dish; set aside.

Cook sausage until browned,
stirring to crumble; drain well.

Combine sausage, eggs, milk,
cheese, and salt in a large mixing bowl; stir well. Pour over
bread cubes. Cover and refrigerate overnight.

Bake, uncovered, at 350° for
50 minutes or until golden
brown and set. Remove from
oven, and garnish with a tomato
rose and fresh parsley sprigs.
Cut into 3-inch squares to
serve. Yield: 12 servings.

FRESH FRUIT SALAD

6 peaches, peeled and cut
  into bite-size pieces
1½ pounds red plums, cut
  into bite-size pieces
½ pound seedless white
  grapes
½ pound seedless red grapes
1 (15½-ounce) can pineapple
  chunks, undrained
½ cup sugar (optional)
Juice of 1 lime
1 teaspoon ground ginger
Fresh mint sprig

Place fruit in a large serving
bowl, tossing gently. Sprinkle
with sugar, if desired. (Sugar
may not be necessary depending
on sweetness of the fruit.) Combine lime juice and ginger in a
small mixing bowl, stirring well.
Pour lime juice mixture over
fruit; toss gently. Cover and
chill. Before serving, garnish
with a sprig of mint. Yield: 12
servings.

Note: Any other fresh fruit
may be added.

U.S. Naval Academy's championship football team of 1893, Annapolis, Maryland.

United States Naval Academy Archives

Almond Puff Coffee Cake is pastry topped with puffy choux paste, baked, iced, and almond encrusted.

ICEBOX POTATO ROLLS

1 package dry yeast
½ cup sugar, divided
½ cup lukewarm water (105°
   to 115°)
1 cup milk, scalded
1 cup cooked, mashed
   potatoes
⅔ cup shortening
1 teaspoon salt
6½ cups all-purpose flour,
   divided
2 eggs, beaten
Butter or margarine, melted

Combine yeast, 1 teaspoon sugar, and lukewarm water in a small mixing bowl; stir well, and let stand 5 minutes or until bubbly.

Combine scalded milk, potatoes, shortening, remaining sugar, and salt in a large mixing bowl; stir until shortening melts. Cool to lukewarm (105° to 115°); stir in yeast mixture and 2 cups flour. Beat until smooth. Cover and let rise in a warm place (85°), free from drafts, 1 hour or until doubled in bulk.

Stir dough down. Add eggs and enough remaining flour to make a soft dough. Turn dough out onto a floured surface; knead 8 minutes or until smooth and elastic. Place dough in a large greased bowl, turning to grease top. Cover and refrigerate overnight.

Punch dough down. Shape into 1½-inch balls; arrange in 2 lightly greased 13- x 9- x 2-inch baking pans. Brush rolls with melted butter. Cover and repeat rising procedure 1 hour or until doubled in bulk. Bake at 400° for 12 to 15 minutes. Remove from pans, and serve warm. Yield: 4 dozen.

ALMOND PUFF COFFEE CAKE

2 cups all-purpose flour,
   divided
½ cup butter or margarine,
   softened
1 cup plus 2 tablespoons
   water, divided
½ cup butter or margarine,
   melted
2½ teaspoons almond
   extract, divided
3 eggs, beaten
1½ cups sifted powdered
   sugar
2 tablespoons butter or
   margarine, softened
1½ tablespoons warm
   water
¼ cup sliced almonds

Place 1 cup flour in a medium mixing bowl; cut in ½ cup butter with a pastry blender until mixture resembles coarse meal. Sprinkle 2 tablespoons water evenly over surface; stir with a fork until dry ingredients are moistened. Shape dough into a ball. Divide ball in half, placing halves on an ungreased baking sheet. Pat each half into a 12- x 3-inch strip, leaving 3 inches between strips.

Combine 1 cup water and melted butter in a medium saucepan; bring to a boil. Add 1 teaspoon almond extract and remaining flour, all at once, stirring vigorously over low heat until mixture leaves sides of pan and forms a smooth ball. Remove from heat, and cool slightly.

Add eggs; beat until batter is smooth. Spread batter evenly over each pastry strip. Bake at 350° for 1 hour. Remove from oven, and keep warm.

Combine powdered sugar, 2 tablespoons butter, remaining almond extract, and 1½ tablespoons warm water in a medium mixing bowl, beating well. Spread over tops of cakes; sprinkle with almonds. Slice and serve warm. Yield: 12 servings.

BEFORE THE WEDDING

Flowers abundant, silver gleaming, napery crisp; a pre-nuptial champagne brunch is nothing if not pretty. Not formal in the rigid sense of the word, the wedding brunch is nevertheless evidence of loving attention to details that are to become part of a couple's memories of their special day. Brunch before an afternoon wedding has all but supplanted the luncheon, in that it may be served at an earlier hour. Service may be from a sideboard with comfortable seating available. Or some of the food, ideally three elements of the menu, may be plated in the kitchen, the rest passed by a helper. Plates are then placed with the main dish facing the guest.

CHAMPAGNE * FRESH JUICE ASSORTMENT
CRABMEAT-STUFFED MUSHROOM CAPS
BROILED TOMATOES
CREAMED EGGS IN TOAST CUPS
PETITE BLUEBERRY MUFFINS
RUM-BUTTER COFFEE CAKE

Serves 10

CRABMEAT-STUFFED MUSHROOM CAPS

24 large mushrooms
3 tablespoons butter or margarine, melted
1 cup fresh crabmeat, drained and flaked
¼ cup butter or margarine
⅓ cup seasoned, dry breadcrumbs
2 tablespoons chopped fresh parsley
¼ teaspoon salt
⅛ teaspoon red pepper
Grated Parmesan cheese

Clean mushrooms with damp paper towels. Remove mushroom stems; chop and set aside 1 cup stems. Dip mushroom caps in melted butter; place caps, top side down, in a shallow roasting pan.

Sauté reserved mushroom stems and crabmeat in ¼ cup butter in a large skillet until tender. Stir in breadcrumbs, parsley, salt, and pepper.

Spoon crabmeat mixture into mushroom caps, and sprinkle with Parmesan cheese. Bake at 350° for 15 minutes. Transfer to a serving platter, and serve hot. Yield: 2 dozen.

BROILED TOMATOES

5 slices bacon, halved
5 medium tomatoes, halved
10 slices Cheddar cheese

Cook bacon in a heavy skillet over medium heat until partially cooked. Drain well on paper towels; set aside.

Cut a thin slice from bottom of each tomato half so it will sit flat; place tomato halves in a shallow roasting pan. Broil 6 inches from heating element 10 minutes. Remove from heat, and place a slice of cheese on each tomato half; top with bacon pieces. Return to oven and broil an additional minute or until cheese melts and bacon is cooked. Serve immediately. Yield: 10 servings.

CREAMED EGGS IN TOAST CUPS

10 slices bread, crust removed
Melted butter or margarine
¼ cup butter or margarine
¼ cup all-purpose flour
1 cup milk
1 cup whipping cream
½ teaspoon salt
4 hard-cooked eggs, coarsely chopped

Roll each slice of bread flat. Brush one side of each slice with melted butter, and press each into an 8-ounce custard cup. Mold bread to side of cup. Bake at 350° for 15 minutes or until lightly browned. Transfer toast cups to a serving platter; set aside.

Melt ¼ cup butter in a heavy saucepan over low heat; add flour, and stir until smooth. Cook 1 minute, stirring constantly. Gradually add milk and whipping cream; cook over medium heat, stirring constantly, until thickened and bubbly. Stir in salt and egg.

Spoon ⅓ cup mixture into each toast cup. Serve immediately. Yield: 10 servings.

A rainbow of juices, Creamed Eggs in Toast Cups, and mo

PETITE BLUEBERRY MUFFINS

1 cup fresh blueberries
1¾ cups self-rising flour,
  divided
½ cup shortening
1 cup sugar
⅔ cup milk
3 tablespoons boiling water
3 eggs, beaten
1 teaspoon vanilla extract
½ teaspoon almond extract

Dredge blueberries in ¼ cup flour; set aside.

Cream shortening and sugar in a large mixing bowl. Add remaining flour, milk, and boiling water; beat at medium speed of an electric mixer 2 minutes. Add eggs and flavorings; beat an additional 2 minutes. Gently fold in dredged blueberries.

Spoon mixture into paper-lined miniature muffin pans. Bake at 375° for 20 to 25 minutes. Remove muffins from pans, and serve immediately. Yield: about 7 dozen.

A breathless moment!
Postcard, 1910.

RUM-BUTTER COFFEE CAKE

1 package dry yeast
1 cup lukewarm milk (105°
  to 115°)
¾ cup butter or margarine,
  divided
¾ cup sugar, divided
2 eggs
4 cups all-purpose flour
1 cup chopped mixed
  candied fruit
Rum-Butter Mixture

Dissolve yeast in milk; let stand 5 minutes. Soften ½ cup butter in a large mixing bowl; beat until smooth. Gradually add ½ cup sugar, beating until light and fluffy. Add eggs, beating well. Add flour and yeast mixture alternately, beginning and ending with flour, stirring well after each addition.

Turn dough out onto a lightly floured surface; knead 5 minutes or until smooth. Place in a greased bowl, turning to grease top. Cover and let rise in a warm place (85°), free from drafts, 1 hour or until doubled in bulk.

Turn dough out onto a lightly floured pastry cloth. Roll into a 23- x 13-inch rectangle. Melt remaining butter; brush on rectangle. Sprinkle with remaining sugar and candied fruit. Roll up jellyroll fashion, beginning at long side; moisten edges to seal.

Pour Rum-Butter Mixture into a well-greased 10-inch tube pan; arrange roll over mixture. Pinch ends together to seal. Cover; repeat rising procedure.

Bake at 350° for 50 minutes. Remove from oven; invert pan, and cool cake. Slice and serve. Yield: one 10-inch cake.

Rum-Butter Mixture:

1 cup firmly packed brown
  sugar
½ cup butter or margarine,
  melted
¼ teaspoon ground cinnamon
¼ teaspoon ground nutmeg
Pinch of ground cloves
3 tablespoons rum

Combine all ingredients in a small mixing bowl, stirring well. Yield: about 1½ cups.

A Texas ladies' club met for card playing at the Rice Hotel, Houston, c.1911.

CANASTA CLUB BRUNCH

If the notion of a Canasta Club brunch seems a little old-fashioned, it is! Years ago, an Alabama-born woman came to Rockdale, Texas, as a child and later lived in Austin for a while. Then, according to her daughter, she moved to Houston to get away from an overabundance of visiting relatives. Somewhere along the way, she developed a passion for card playing. At frequent intervals, she and her friends gathered for bridge, or, especially, canasta. They loved good food as well as a good game; delicious meals combined well with avid gamesmanship. They still go together. Enjoy the cold fresh Tomato Juice Salad while the soufflé bakes. Viva Canasta!

TOMATO JUICE SALAD
CHEESE SOUFFLÉ
TOASTED DOUGHNUTS
BACON AND CANADIAN BACON
THIN TOAST SLICES
STRAWBERRY PRESERVES

Serves 8

CHEESE SOUFFLÉ

¼ cup plus 2 tablespoons
  butter or margarine
¼ cup plus 2 tablespoons
  all-purpose flour
2 cups milk
1 teaspoon salt
½ teaspoon white
  pepper
7 eggs, separated
1 (3-ounce) can sliced
  mushrooms, drained
  and chopped
2 cups (8 ounces) shredded
  sharp Cheddar cheese

Lightly butter a 2-quart soufflé dish. Cut a piece of aluminum foil long enough to circle
the dish, allowing a 1-inch over-
lap. Fold foil lengthwise into
thirds, and lightly butter one
side. Wrap foil around dish, buttered side against dish, allowing
it to extend 3 inches above rim.
Secure foil with string. Set prepared dish aside.

Melt butter in a medium
saucepan over low heat; add
flour, stirring until smooth.
Cook 1 minute, stirring constantly. Gradually add milk;
cook over medium heat, stirring
constantly, until mixture is
thickened and bubbly. Stir in
salt and pepper; remove from
heat, and set aside to cool
slightly.

Beat egg yolks in a large mixing bowl until thick and lemon
colored; add cooled sauce, mixing well with a wire whisk. Add
chopped mushrooms and
cheese, mixing well.

Beat egg whites (at room temperature) until stiff but not dry.
Stir 1 cup beaten egg whites
into sauce mixture. Gently fold
remaining egg whites into
sauce.

Spoon mixture into prepared
soufflé dish. Bake at 375° for 45
minutes. Remove collar; serve
immediately. Yield: 8 servings.

*Tomato Juice Salad starts
a card party brunch:
Bacon and Canadian
Bacon, Cheese Soufflé,
and Toasted Doughnuts.*

TOMATO JUICE
SALAD

1 clove garlic
1 (24-ounce) can tomato juice
4 medium tomatoes, unpeeled
  and chopped
8 finely chopped green onions
2 cucumbers, peeled and
  finely chopped
1 cup finely chopped celery
2 tablespoons vinegar
2 tablespoons lemon juice
1 tablespoon salt
Dash of pepper

Rub a large glass or ceramic
bowl with garlic clove; discard
garlic. Place remaining ingredients in bowl, mixing well.
Cover tightly, and chill overnight. Serve in individual
bowls. Yield: about 12 cups.

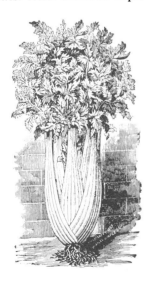

TOASTED
DOUGHNUTS

1 cup sugar
2 tablespoons shortening,
  melted
2 eggs
½ cup milk
3 cups all-purpose flour
2 teaspoons baking powder
½ teaspoon ground nutmeg
¼ teaspoon salt
Vegetable oil
¼ cup butter or margarine,
  melted
Sifted powdered sugar
  (optional)

Combine sugar and melted
shortening in a large mixing
bowl; mix well. Add eggs and
milk; beat well.

Combine flour, baking powder, nutmeg, and salt; add to
creamed mixture, stirring well.
Turn dough out onto a heavily
floured surface; roll to ¼-inch
thickness. Cut dough with a
floured doughnut cutter.

Drop doughnuts, a few at a
time, into deep hot oil (375°).
Fry until golden brown, turning
once. Drain doughnuts well on
paper towels.

Split doughnuts in half crosswise. Place on baking sheets cut
side up; brush with butter.

Broil 4 inches from heating
element 2 minutes or until
lighty browned. Sprinkle
doughnut halves with powdered
sugar, if desired. Yield: about
1½ dozen.

NEW YEAR'S EVE MIDNIGHT BRUNCH

Precedent for a New Year's Eve midnight brunch goes back hundreds of years. But to find it, we must look under "supper" and "breakfast." In Colonial days, when a grand ball was given, people knew how to party. They danced half the night and then ate a prodigious meal called supper. Similar menus were served in the homes of planters for breakfast after the farm work was underway. Mary F. Henderson wrote of huge "company breakfasts" in 1876. If all these people had had the word brunch, they surely would have used it. New Year's revelry inspires the appetite, so don't hang back; get some help in the kitchen and give the New Year a super send-off.

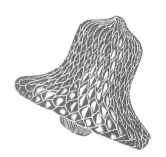

FRESH FRUIT IN SEASON
or
HOT CARAMEL FRUIT
ROAST FILLET OF BEEF
COUNTRY HAM
OYSTER OMELET
FRIED GRITS
TINY BISCUITS
HOT CHOCOLATE

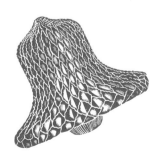

Serves 8

An Alfred S. Ames and Company celebration, St. Charles Hotel, New Orleans, c.1927.

HOT CARAMEL FRUIT

2 (29-ounce) cans sliced
  peaches, undrained
1 (16-ounce) can sweet dark
  pitted cherries, drained
2 (6-ounce) packages dried
  apricots
12 pitted dates, coarsely
  chopped
¼ teaspoon grated lemon
  rind
¼ teaspoon grated orange
  rind
Juice of half a lemon
Juice of half an orange
1 cup firmly packed brown
  sugar
12 walnut halves

Combine peaches, cherries,
apricots, dates, rind, and juice
in a large mixing bowl. Stir in
brown sugar. Pour into a lightly
greased 3-quart casserole.

Arrange walnut halves over top
of fruit. Cover mixture, and refrigerate overnight.

Let stand at room temperature at least 1 hour. Cover and
bake at 325° for 1 hour. Serve
hot. Yield: 8 to 10 servings.

ROAST FILLET
OF BEEF

½ cup butter or margarine
1½ tablespoons
  Worcestershire sauce
3 tablespoons red wine
  vinegar
1 (2- to 2½-pound) beef
  tenderloin, trimmed
6 cloves garlic
Fresh parsley sprigs (optional)

Combine butter, Worcestershire sauce, and vinegar in a
saucepan. Cook over low heat

until butter melts; stir often.
Remove from heat; keep warm.

Make 6 small slits in tenderloin; stuff each slit with a garlic
clove. Place tenderloin on a
lightly greased rack in a shallow
roasting pan. Tuck narrow end
under to make roast more uni-
formly thick. Insert meat thermometer, if desired. Bake,
uncovered, at 350° for 40 minutes or until meat thermometer
registers 140° (rare), basting
often with prepared sauce.

Remove and discard garlic.
Cut tenderloin into ½-inch-
thick slices; arrange on a warm
serving platter. Garnish with
parsley sprigs, if desired; serve
immediately. Yield: 8 servings.

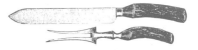

COUNTRY HAM

1 (10-pound) country ham
1 cup vinegar
1¼ cups firmly packed brown
 sugar, divided
1 cup molasses

Wash ham, scrubbing thoroughly with a stiff brush; rinse well. Place ham in a very large container; cover with cold water. Soak overnight. Drain.

Combine vinegar, 1 cup brown sugar, and molasses in a large mixing bowl. Place ham in a large roasting pan. Pour vinegar mixture over ham, and add enough cold water to cover ham. Cover and bake at 500° until vinegar mixture boils; reduce heat to 300°, and bake 2½ hours, allowing 15 minutes per pound. Turn oven off, and allow ham to cool in oven overnight. Do not open oven door.

Remove ham from pan; remove skin and discard. Place ham, fat side up, in a shallow roasting pan; sprinkle remaining brown sugar over ham. Bake at 325° for 30 minutes or until browned. Transfer to a serving platter. Cool completely. Cut into thin slices to serve. Yield: 8 servings.

Note: Reserve remaining ham for other uses.

OYSTER OMELET

1 (12-ounce) container
 Standard oysters,
 undrained
3½ tablespoons butter or
 margarine, divided
1½ tablespoons all-purpose
 flour
Pinch of baking soda
3 tablespoons whipping
 cream
½ teaspoon salt, divided
¼ teaspoon pepper, divided
3 eggs
¼ cup milk

Drain oysters, reserving 3 tablespoons oyster liquor. Chop 4 oysters; set remaining oysters and oyster liquor aside.

Melt 1½ tablespoons butter in a heavy saucepan over low heat; add flour, stirring until smooth. Cook 1 minute, stirring constantly. Dissolve soda in whipping cream; gradually stir into flour mixture with reserved oyster liquor. Cook over medium heat, stirring constantly, until thickened and bubbly. Stir in chopped oysters, ¼ teaspoon salt, and ⅛ teaspoon pepper. Set aside, and keep warm.

Melt remaining butter in an 8-inch omelet pan or heavy skillet over medium heat; add reserved oysters, and sauté 1 minute. Drain oysters; set aside and keep warm.

Combine eggs, milk, remaining salt, and pepper in a small mixing bowl; beat well. Pour egg mixture into omelet pan or skillet. Cook over medium heat, lifting edges of omelet and tilting pan to allow uncooked portion of omelet to flow underneath.

Cook until egg mixture is set and no longer flows freely; place reserved sautéed oysters over half of omelet. Fold omelet in half over oysters; transfer to a warm serving platter. Serve immediately with reserved oyster sauce. Yield: 2 servings.

Note: Repeat procedure for additional servings.

*A 1909 postcard
brings New Year's greetings.*

Oyster Omelet with Fried Grits and Hot Caramel Fruit.

TINY BISCUITS

2½ cups all-purpose flour
2 teaspoons baking powder
1 teaspoon salt
¼ teaspoon baking soda
½ cup shortening or lard
¾ cup buttermilk
1 egg, beaten

Combine flour, baking powder, salt, and soda in a large mixing bowl; stir well. Cut in shortening with a pastry blender until mixture resembles coarse meal. Combine buttermilk and egg, beating well; gradually add to dry ingredients, stirring just until moistened.

Turn dough out onto a lightly floured surface, and knead 10 to 12 times.

Roll dough to ½-inch thickness; cut with a 1½-inch biscuit cutter. Place biscuits on a lightly greased baking sheet. Bake at 450° for 12 minutes or until lightly browned. Serve hot. Yield: 3½ dozen.

HOT CHOCOLATE

⅔ cup sugar
2 teaspoons cornstarch
2 quarts milk, divided
½ cup boiling water
⅛ teaspoon salt
4 (1-ounce) squares
    semisweet chocolate, melted
Whipped cream

Combine sugar and cornstarch in a small mixing bowl, mixing well. Add 1 cup milk, stirring well. Scald remaining milk in top of a large double boiler over simmering water. Add sugar mixture; cook 10 minutes, stirring constantly.

Gradually add boiling water and salt to melted chocolate; stirring until smooth. Add chocolate mixture to milk mixture in top of double boiler. Beat with a wire whisk until frothy. Serve immediately in mugs with a dollop of whipped cream. Yield: 8 servings.

FRIED GRITS

1 quart water
1½ teaspoons salt, divided
1 cup uncooked quick
    grits
1 cup all-purpose flour
¼ teaspoon pepper
¾ cup milk
1 egg, beaten
Lard

Bring water and ½ teaspoon salt to a boil in a large saucepan; stir in grits. Cook grits until done, following package directions. Remove from heat.

Pour cooked grits into a greased 8½- x 4½- x 3-inch loafpan. Cool; cover and refrigerate overnight.

Remove chilled grits by inverting pan; cut loaf into ½-inch slices, and set aside.

Combine flour, remaining salt, pepper, milk, and egg in a small mixing bowl; mix well. Dip slices into batter.

Melt lard in a large skillet at 325° to a depth of ½ inch; add grits slices, and cook 5 minutes or until golden brown, turning once. Serve immediately. Yield: 8 servings.

MEDLEY OF RECIPES

A sunny window lights up a Southern-style brunch (clockwise from left): Cranberry Cooler (page 92) with Baked Eggs (page 118), Sausage-Apple Cornbread (page 131), Apricot Nut Bread (page 102), and applesauce.

"Mellow bourbon, aged in oaken barrels . . . granulated sugar slowly mixed into chilled limestone water to make a silvery mixture as smooth as some rare Egyptian oil. . . ." This is part of statesman Henry Clay's recipe for Kentucky mint juleps; he was so partial to it that he recorded it in his diary. No serious observer of the early American South forebore to mention the Southerner's propensity for strong drink. In 1774, a visitor wrote that the planter rose early and had his drink "because a julep before breakfast was believed to give protection against malaria."

After inspecting his stock, the planter was ready to join family and guests for a hearty ten o'clock breakfast. It is safe to say that no people anywhere have been habituated to such expansive breakfast menus as were the Southerners of earlier days: chicken, bacon, ham, eggs, hominy, biscuits, fried apples, vegetables, fried cornmeal mush, and more. Shrimp gravy with grits was a coastal specialty. But pie for breakfast was a Northern phenomenon that slowly moved South.

The adult male's medicinal draught was not the only morning beverage available. Chocolate, tea, and coffee all were popular; homes with flexible budgets served all three. Good hotels listed tea, both green and black, coffee, boiled milk, and chocolate.

Waffles were made possible and popular after the waffle iron was introduced from Belgium by Thomas Jefferson. By 1824, Mary Randolph's *The Virginia Housewife* was able to include "Rice Woffles," as well as four kinds of fritters.

Game was popular breakfast food on plantations like Catalpa, near St. Francisville, Louisiana. Built by William J. Fort in the early 1800s, ruined by the Civil War, and burned down late in the century, Catalpa's mansion was replaced by a Victorian cottage. Mamie Fort Thompson and her husband, James, still own the place, which has never been out of the Fort family. Fried squirrel and "beat" biscuit or broiled quail followed by sweet Creole cream cheese are among her family recipes. "Grandfather used to say the best part of the turkey was hash and grits the next day for breakfast," Mrs. Thompson recalled. Some old, some updated, here are recipes for some memorable breakfasts and brunches.

CHASE & SANBORN'S "SEAL BRAND" COFFEE

SERVED EXCLUSIVELY AT THE WORLD'S FAIR.

Foldover ad card for Chase and Sanborn's coffee, 1893.

EYE-OPENERS

A GOOD CUP OF COFFEE

8 cups cold water
¾ cup regular grind coffee

Pour cold water into percolator. Place coffee in basket. Let coffee begin to percolate over high heat; reduce heat, and let percolate 5 minutes or until coffee reaches desired strength. Yield: about 8 cups.

COFFEE FOR A CROWD

2 gallons water
1 pound regular grind coffee
1 muslin bag

Bring water to a boil in a stainless steel stockpot. Place coffee in muslin bag; tie loosely. Place bag in boiling water. Cover and remove from heat; let stand 10 minutes. Uncover and carefully dip bag up and down until coffee reaches desired strength. Remove bag; discard. Cover stockpot, and keep warm over low heat until ready to serve.

Ladle hot coffee into a warm coffee pot. Serve immediately. Yield: 2 gallons.

ICED COFFEE

10 cups coffee, divided

Cool coffee to room temperature; chill.

Pour 2 cups chilled coffee into two ice cube trays, and freeze until firm.

Place frozen coffee cubes in serving glasses; pour remaining chilled coffee over cubes. Serve immediately. Yield: 8 servings.

GOOD TEA

1 tablespoon plus 1 teaspoon tea leaves
1 quart boiling water
Milk
Sugar
Lemon slices

Place tea leaves in a 1-quart glass pitcher; slowly pour boiling water over tea leaves. Cover and steep 5 minutes.

Strain and discard tea leaves. Serve hot tea in individual cups with milk, sugar, and lemon slices. Yield: 1 quart.

Note: To prepare iced tea, let hot tea come to room temperature; chill. Serve chilled tea over crushed ice.

SPICED TEA

3 quarts water
1 teaspoon whole cloves
3 (3-inch) sticks cinnamon
6 regular tea bags
1½ cups sugar
2 cups water
Juice of 3 oranges
Juice of 3 lemons
Orange slices (optional)

Combine water, cloves, and cinnamon in a large stainless steel Dutch oven; bring to a boil. Remove from heat, and add tea bags; cover and steep 15 minutes. Discard tea bags, cloves, and cinnamon; set tea aside.

Combine sugar, water, and juice in a small stainless steel saucepan; bring to a boil, stirring frequently until sugar dissolves. Combine tea mixture and juice mixture, stirring until well blended. Pour into serving cups, and garnish with orange slices, if desired. Serve hot. Yield: about 3½ quarts.

MULLED CIDER

2 quarts apple cider
2 tablespoons firmly packed brown sugar
2 (3-inch) sticks cinnamon
1 teaspoon whole cloves
⅛ teaspoon ground cloves
1 orange, sliced and seeded

Combine all ingredients in a medium Dutch oven; place over medium heat. Simmer, uncovered, 2 hours. Strain and serve hot in mugs. Yield: 1 quart.

This cozy breakfast for two features the latest General Electric toaster as well as a pot warmer for a steaming hot morning beverage.

OLD-FASHIONED HOT CHOCOLATE

⅓ cup sugar
¼ cup cocoa
1 tablespoon all-purpose flour
1 cup water
1½ cups milk
¼ teaspoon vanilla extract
Pinch of salt
Marshmallows

Combine sugar, cocoa, and flour in a medium saucepan, stirring well. Add water; bring to a boil, stirring frequently. Remove from heat; stir in milk, vanilla, and salt. Cook over medium heat, stirring constantly, until hot.

Place marshmallows in individual cups; fill with hot chocolate. Serve immediately. Yield: 2½ cups.

CHOCOLATE FLUFF

4 eggs, separated
3 cups milk
¾ cup chocolate syrup
1 tablespoon plus 1 teaspoon sugar
Ground nutmeg

Beat egg yolks in a large mixing bowl until thick and lemon colored. Stir in milk and chocolate syrup, mixing well. Set mixture aside.

Beat egg whites (at room temperature) in a medium mixing bowl until foamy. Gradually add sugar, beating until stiff peaks form. Gently fold egg whites into reserved milk mixture, blending well. Pour mixture into chilled serving glasses, and sprinkle tops with ground nutmeg. Yield: 4 servings.

CRANBERRY COOLER

1 quart cranberry juice cocktail
1 cup orange juice
1 cup pineapple juice
1 cup water
⅓ cup lemon juice
Ice cubes

Combine first 5 ingredients in a large bowl; chill thoroughly. Pour cranberry cooler over ice in serving glasses. Serve immediately. Yield: about 2 quarts.

HOT SPICED TOMATO JUICE

1 bay leaf
1½ teaspoons whole allspice
¼ cup water
1 (46-ounce) can tomato juice
1½ teaspoons sugar
1½ teaspoons salt
2 tablespoons lemon juice
1½ teaspoons Worcestershire sauce
Dash of hot sauce

Combine bay leaf, allspice, and water in a small saucepan; place over medium heat, and bring to a boil. Cook 5 minutes.

Pour tomato juice into a 2-quart stainless steel saucepan, place over medium heat. Strain spice mixture into tomato juice. Discard whole spices.

Add sugar, salt, lemon juice, Worcestershire sauce, and hot sauce to tomato juice mixture; stir well. Cook over medium heat until thoroughly heated. Pour into serving cups, and serve hot. Yield: 1½ quarts.

Old-Fashioned Hot Chocolate is better with marshmallows dropped into the cup before the chocolate is poured.

MORNING CALL

3 tablespoons lime juice
3 tablespoons maraschino
  cherry juice
1½ ounces Pernod or other
  licorice-flavored liqueur
Crushed ice
Lime wedge
Maraschino cherry

Combine juice and Pernod, stirring well. Pour over crushed ice in a serving glass.

Garnish with a lime wedge and maraschino cherry. Yield: 1 serving.

MIMOSA

2 cups orange juice, chilled
2 cups brut champagne,
  chilled

Combine juice and champagne in a 1-quart pitcher; stir well. Pour over ice in tall champagne glasses, and serve. Yield: 1 quart.

ORANGE BLOSSOM

1 ounce gin
1 ounce French vermouth
2 tablespoons orange
  juice
Ice cubes

Combine gin, vermouth, and orange juice; stir well. Pour over ice in serving glasses. Yield: 1 serving.

SALTY DOG

¾ cup plus 1 tablespoon
  grapefruit juice, divided
1 tablespoon coarse salt
Ice cubes
1½ ounces vodka

Dip rim of glass in 1 tablespoon grapefruit juice; dip in a shallow dish of coarse salt to coat rim of glass. Fill serving glass with ice cubes; pour vodka and remaining grapefruit juice over ice. Stir and serve immediately. Yield: 1 serving.

MARGARITA

¼ cup plus 1 tablespoon
  lime juice,
  divided
Coarse salt
1½ ounces tequila
¾ ounce Triple Sec
1 teaspoon sugar
Crushed ice
Lime wedge (optional)

Dip rim of cocktail glass in 1 tablespoon lime juice; dip in a shallow dish of coarse salt to coat rim of glass.

Combine remaining ¼ cup lime juice, tequila, Triple Sec, and sugar in a small pitcher, mixing well. Pour mixture over crushed ice in prepared glass. Garnish with a lime wedge, if desired. Yield: 1 serving.

CLARET LEMONADE

⅓ cup sugar
½ cup freshly squeezed
  lemon juice
½ cup claret or other dry red
  wine
1 (28-ounce) bottle club soda,
  chilled
Crushed ice
Lemon slices

Combine sugar, lemon juice, and wine in a large pitcher; stir until sugar dissolves. Stir in club soda; pour over crushed ice in serving glasses. Garnish with lemon slices, and serve. Yield: about 1 quart.

Peach slices garnish Scarlett O'Hara (front). Lemon goes with Claret Lemonade.

SCARLETT O'HARA

1 (16-ounce) package frozen
  sliced peaches, slightly
  thawed
½ cup sugar
½ cup bourbon
¼ cup plus 2 tablespoons
  sweetened lime juice
4 cups crushed ice
Additional peach slices

Place half of peaches in container of an electric blender; process until smooth. Add remaining peaches, sugar, bourbon, and lime juice; process until smooth. Add crushed ice; process until thick and slushy.

Pour into glasses; garnish with peach slices. Serve immediately. Yield: about 6 cups.

BLOODY MARY

1½ cups chopped celery
1 cup chopped cucumbers
¼ cup chopped onion
1 teaspoon dried parsley
  flakes
1 teaspoon lemon juice
¼ teaspoon Worcestershire
  sauce
¼ teaspoon steak sauce
¼ teaspoon dry mustard
¼ teaspoon garlic salt
¼ teaspoon salt
¼ teaspoon pepper
1 (46-ounce) can tomato
  juice, divided
2 bay leaves
1 cup vodka
Ice cubes
Celery stalks

Combine first 11 ingredients in container of an electric blender; add 1 cup tomato juice, and process until smooth.

Pour vegetable mixture and remaining tomato juice into a large pitcher, stirring well to blend. Add bay leaves, and chill several hours.

Remove bay leaves; stir in vodka. Pour over ice cubes in serving glasses; garnish with celery stalks. Yield: about 2 quarts.

MILK PUNCH

1 cup milk
½ cup brandy
1 tablespoon sugar
Crushed ice
Ground nutmeg

Combine milk, brandy, and sugar in a tall glass; stir until sugar dissolves. Add crushed ice to fill glass. Sprinkle with nutmeg. Yield: 1 serving.

MORNING EGGNOG

6 eggs, separated
1¼ cups sugar, divided
1 quart milk
¾ cup bourbon
⅓ cup light rum
2 cups whipping cream
Ground nutmeg

Beat egg yolks in a large mixing bowl until thick and lemon colored. Gradually add ½ cup sugar, beating constantly. Stir in milk, bourbon, and rum, blending well.

Beat egg whites (at room temperature) in a large mixing bowl until foamy. Gradually add ½ cup sugar, 1 tablespoon at a time, beating until stiff peaks form. Gently fold egg whites into milk mixture, blending well.

Beat whipping cream until foamy; gradually add remaining sugar, 2 tablespoons at a time, beating until soft peaks form. Fold whipped cream into milk mixture. Ladle into serving cups, and sprinkle each serving with nutmeg. Yield: 1 gallon.

CHAMPAGNE PUNCH

1 (8¼-ounce) can sliced
  pineapple, undrained
2 cups water
½ cup sifted powdered
  sugar
⅔ cup orange juice
¼ cup plus 2 tablespoons
  lemon juice
2 cups Chablis or other dry
  white wine, chilled
1 (25.4-ounce) bottle
  champagne, chilled
Ice ring (optional)

Drain pineapple, reserving juice; set aside. Reserve pineapple rings to assemble ice ring, if desired.

Combine water and sugar, stirring until sugar dissolves. Add orange juice, lemon juice, and reserved pineapple juice; mix well.

Pour juice mixture into a punch bowl; add wine and champagne just before serving. Garnish with an ice ring, if desired. Serve immediately. Yield: about 2½ quarts.

Recipes for single drinks usually do not translate well into quantity service. However, there are times, admitted W.C. Whitfield in *Here's How*, "when a liquid structure that will withstand the attacks of 10, 12, or even 50 of your thirst-maddened friends must be prepared . . . Christmas, the Year's birthday, the return of the Prodigal Son, the departure of the Nuptialed Daughter, the arrival of twins. . . ." A brunch guest list may grow so large that only bowls or pitchers full of liquid refreshment will serve.

MOTHER THOMAS' CORN LIGHT BREAD

1 teaspoon baking soda
1 cup buttermilk
1 cup sugar
1 cup cornmeal
1 cup all-purpose flour
2 teaspoons salt
1 egg, lightly beaten
1 tablespoon lard, melted
¼ cup bacon drippings, divided

Dissolve soda in buttermilk, stirring well; set aside. Combine sugar, cornmeal, flour, and salt in a medium mixing bowl; mix well. Add buttermilk mixture, egg, and lard, stirring well.

Pour batter into a well-greased 8½- x 4½- x 3-inch loaf-pan. Bake at 350° for 50 minutes or until a wooden pick inserted in center comes out clean. Cool in pan 10 minutes; remove bread from pan, and cool completely on a wire rack.

Slice bread into ½-inch-thick slices; set aside. Heat 1 tablespoon bacon drippings in a large skillet over high heat; add bread slices to fill skillet. Cook until golden brown on both sides, turning once. Repeat procedure with remaining bread slices and bacon drippings. Serve hot. Yield: 8 servings.

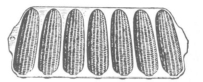

CRUNCHY CORN STICKS

½ cup butter or margarine, melted and divided
1 cup self-rising cornmeal
½ cup all-purpose flour
1 cup buttermilk
1 egg, beaten

Brush cast-iron corn stick pans lightly with a small amount of melted butter, and set aside.

Combine cornmeal and flour in a small mixing bowl; mix well. Add buttermilk and egg, stirring just until dry ingredients are moistened. Stir remaining butter into batter, mixing well.

Heat prepared pans in a 400° oven 3 minutes or until very hot. Spoon batter into pans, filling two-thirds full. Bake at 400° for 20 minutes or until lightly browned. Remove corn sticks from pans immediately, and serve hot. Yield: 1 dozen.

GRANDMA'S BEST BUTTERMILK BISCUITS

3½ cups self-rising flour
1 tablespoon plus 1½ teaspoons baking powder
½ cup plus 1 tablespoon shortening
1½ cups plus 2 tablespoons buttermilk

Combine flour and baking powder in a large mixing bowl, stirring well. Cut in shortening with a pastry blender until the mixture resembles coarse meal. Gradually add buttermilk, stirring until dry ingredients are moistened.

Turn dough out onto a floured surface, and knead 4 to 5 times.

Roll dough to ½-inch thickness; cut with a 2¾-inch biscuit cutter. Place biscuits on a greased baking sheet. Bake at 425° for 12 minutes or until biscuits are lightly browned. Yield: 1½ dozen.

CREAM BISCUITS

2 cups all-purpose flour
1½ teaspoons baking powder
¼ teaspoon salt
1½ teaspoons shortening
1 cup plus 2 tablespoons whipping cream

Combine flour, baking powder, and salt; sift together 3 times. Cut in shortening with a pastry blender until mixture resembles coarse meal. Sprinkle whipping cream over flour mixture; stir until dry ingredients are moistened.

Turn dough out onto a lightly floured surface, and dust top of dough with flour.

Roll dough to ¾-inch thickness; cut with a 2¼-inch biscuit cutter. Place biscuits on a greased baking sheet. Bake at 450° for 12 minutes or until lightly browned. Yield: 1 dozen.

Pretty label from yesteryear: corn flour, 1890.

Collection of Business Americana

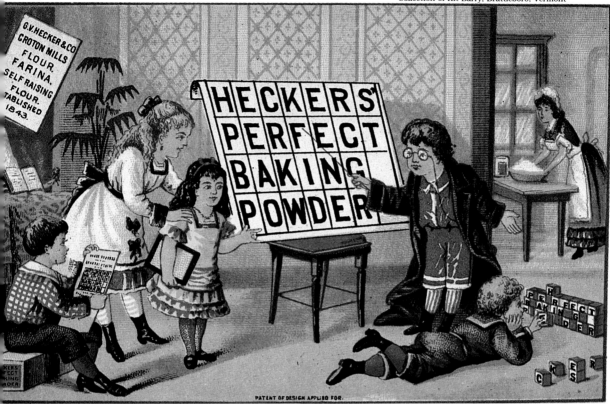

, play-school project is ne way to learn spelling. n 1890s trade card for eckers' Baking Powder.

SOUR CREAM BISCUITS

cups self-rising flour
2 cup butter or margarine, softened
(8-ounce) carton commercial sour cream

Place flour in a medium mixing bowl. Cut in butter with a astry blender until mixture resembles coarse meal. Gradually dd sour cream, stirring until ry ingredients are moistened. Dough will be stiff.)

Turn dough out onto a lightly oured surface, and knead 10 to 2 times.

Roll dough to ½-inch thickess, and cut with a 1¾-inch iscuit cutter. Place biscuits on greased baking sheet. Bake at 50° for 12 minutes or until ghtly browned. Yield: about 1 ozen.

CHEDDAR CHEESE BISCUITS

1½ cups all-purpose flour
2 teaspoons baking powder
¼ teaspoon salt
¼ cup plus 2 tablespoons shortening
½ cup (2 ounces) shredded sharp Cheddar cheese
⅔ cup milk

Combine flour, baking powder, and salt in a medium mixing bowl; stir well. Cut in shortening until mixture resembles coarse meal. Add cheese; stir well. Sprinkle milk evenly over flour mixture, stirring until dry ingredients are moistened.

Turn dough out onto a floured surface; knead 4 to 5 times.

Roll dough to ½-inch thickness on a lightly floured surface; cut with a 2-inch biscuit cutter. Place biscuits on a greased baking sheet. Bake at 450° for 10 minutes or until lightly browned. Serve hot. Yield: about 1½ dozen.

SWEET POTATO BISCUITS

1½ cups all-purpose flour
1 tablespoon plus 1 teaspoon baking powder
½ teaspoon salt
1¼ cups cooked, mashed sweet potatoes
¼ cup shortening
¼ cup sugar

Sift together flour, baking powder, and salt in a medium mixing bowl. Combine sweet potatoes, shortening, and sugar; mix well. Cut into dry ingredients with a pastry blender until well blended.

Turn dough out onto a lightly floured surface, and knead 4 to 5 times.

Roll dough to ½-inch thickness; cut with a 2-inch biscuit cutter. Place biscuits on greased baking sheets. Bake at 425° for 15 minutes or until lightly browned. Remove from baking sheets, and serve warm. Yield: about 2 dozen.

Whole Wheat Biscuits with Honey Butter. Whatever else is for breakfast, this combo is a winner.

CREAM CHEESE WAFERS

½ cup butter or margarine, softened
4 ounces cream cheese, softened
1 cup biscuit mix

Cream butter and crear cheese in a small mixing bov until fluffy; stir in biscuit mix Chill until firm.

Roll dough on a heavil floured surface to ½-inch thick ness; cut with a 1½-inch biscui cutter. Place wafers on a lightl greased baking sheet.

Bake 350° for 25 minutes c until lightly browned. Serve hc or cold. Yield: 2 dozen.

CHEESE WAFERS

8 ounces sharp Cheddar cheese, shredded
1 cup butter or margarine, softened
2 cups plus 2 tablespoons all-purpose flour
½ teaspoon salt
½ teaspoon paprika

Combine Cheddar cheese an butter in a large mixing bow beat until smooth. Add flou salt, and paprika, stirring wel

Shape dough into ½-inc balls; gently press each to ¼ inch thickness. Place wafers inch apart on lightly grease baking sheets. Bake at 450° fc 7 to 8 minutes. Remove wafer immediately from bakin sheets, and place on wire rack to cool. Yield: 4 dozen.

WHOLE WHEAT BISCUITS WITH HONEY BUTTER

2 cups whole wheat flour
1 tablespoon firmly packed brown sugar
2 teaspoons baking powder
1 teaspoon salt
⅓ cup shortening
1 cup milk
Honey Butter

Combine flour, sugar, baking powder, and salt in a medium mixing bowl; stir well. Cut in shortening with a pastry blender until mixture resembles coarse meal. Gradually add milk, stirring until dry ingredients are moistened.

Turn dough out onto a lightly floured surface, and knead lightly 4 to 5 times.

Roll dough to ½-inch thickness; cut with a 2¼-inch biscuit cutter. Place biscuits on an ungreased baking sheet. Bake at 450° for 10 to 12 minutes. Serve hot with Honey Butter. Yield: 1 dozen.

Honey Butter:

½ cup butter or margarine, softened
½ cup honey

Cream butter in a small mixing bowl until fluffy; gradually add honey, beating well. Yield: about 1 cup.

POPOVERS

1 cup milk
1 cup bread flour
2 eggs
1 tablespoon butter or
   margarine, melted
¼ teaspoon salt

Combine milk and flour in a
small mixing bowl; mix well.
Add eggs, one at a time, beating
well after each addition. Add
butter and salt to milk mixture;
beat 5 minutes.

Heat a well-greased muffin
pan in a 450° oven 3 minutes or
until very hot. Spoon batter into
muffin pans, filling two-thirds
full. Bake at 425° for 20 minutes; reduce heat to 350°, and
bake an additional 20 minutes.
Remove popovers from pan, and
serve immediately. Yield: about
8 popovers.

OATMEAL MUFFINS

1 cup quick-cooking oats,
   uncooked
1 cup buttermilk
1 egg, beaten
1 cup all-purpose flour
½ cup firmly packed brown
   sugar
1 teaspoon baking
   powder
½ teaspoon baking
   soda
1 teaspoon salt
½ cup butter or
   margarine, melted and
   cooled

Combine oats and buttermilk
in a medium mixing bowl; let
stand 30 minutes.

Add next 6 ingredients to oats
mixture, mixing well. Stir in
melted butter.

Spoon batter into greased
muffin pans, filling two-thirds
full. Bake at 400° for 25 minutes
or until golden brown. Cool
slightly; remove from pan, and
serve warm. Yield: 1 dozen.

PEANUT BUTTER MUFFINS

¼ cup shortening
¼ cup creamy peanut butter
½ cup sugar
1 egg
1½ cups all-purpose flour
2 teaspoons baking powder
½ teaspoon salt
½ cup milk
Grape jelly (optional)

Combine shortening and peanut butter in a medium mixing
bowl, stirring well. Gradually
add sugar, beating until light
and fluffy. Add egg, and beat
until well blended.

Combine flour, baking powder, and salt in a small mixing
bowl; add to creamed mixture
alternately with milk, beginning
and ending with flour mixture.
Stir well after each addition.

Spoon batter into greased
muffin pans, filling two-thirds
full. Bake at 350° for 20 minutes
or until lightly browned. Cool
slightly in pans; remove from
pans, and serve warm with jelly,
if desired. Yield: 1 dozen.

Maryland boys testing Smoker's Peanut Butter, c.1910.

Maryland State Archives

BLUEBERRY MUFFINS

2 tablespoons butter,
  softened
2 tablespoons shortening
⅓ cup sugar
1 egg
1½ cups plus 2 tablespoons
  all-purpose flour
1 tablespoon baking
  powder
½ teaspoon salt
¼ cup milk
⅔ cup frozen blueberries,
  thawed and drained

Cream butter and shortening in a large mixing bowl; gradually add sugar, beating until light and fluffy. Add egg, and beat well.

Sift together flour, baking powder, and salt. Add flour mixture to creamed mixture alternately with ¾ cup milk, beginning and ending with the flour mixture.

Spoon batter into a lightly greased and floured muffin pan, filling three-fourths full. Sprinkle blueberries evenly over batter in each muffin cup. Bake at 375° for 25 to 30 minutes or until lightly browned. Remove muffins from pan immediately. Serve warm. Yield: 1 dozen.

ROBERT MORRIS INN CRANBERRY MUFFINS

½ teaspoon grated orange
  rind
¼ cup plus 2 tablespoons
  orange juice
1 egg, beaten
2 tablespoons butter or
  margarine, melted
1 cup all-purpose flour
½ cup sugar
¾ teaspoon baking powder
¼ teaspoon baking soda
½ teaspoon salt
½ cup chopped fresh
  cranberries
¼ cup chopped pecans

Combine orange rind, juice, egg, and butter in a small mixing bowl, mixing well; set aside.

Combine flour, sugar, baking powder, soda, and salt in a medium mixing bowl. Make a well in center of dry ingredients; pour in orange juice mixture. Stir just until dry ingredients are moistened. Gently fold in cranberries and pecans.

Spoon batter into greased muffin pans, filling two-thirds full. Bake at 350° for 25 minutes. Remove from pans, and serve warm. Yield: 1 dozen.

The Robert Morris Inn at Oxford, Maryland, is an outstanding example of eighteenth-century architecture. Built before 1710 by ship's carpenters, it contains hand-hewn beams, ships' nails, and pegged paneling. Morris lived in the house from 1738, when he came to look after the interests of an English trading company, until he was killed in 1750 by wadding from guns being fired in his honor. His son, Robert Morris, Jr., a friend of Washington, was director of finance for the Continental Army. Enlarged several times, the inn is now owned by the Ken Gibsons who keep traditions alive, dispensing comfort and excellent food.

The Robert Morris Inn on the Tred Avon River in Maryland is still favored by travelers. Photo c.1910.

...eberry (front), Peanut Butter, and Robert Morris Inn Cranberry Muffins (rear).

APRICOT NUT BREAD

1 (6-ounce) package dried
    apricots
1 cup sugar
2 tablespoons shortening
1 egg
½ cup orange juice
¼ cup water
2 cups all-purpose flour,
    divided
2 teaspoons baking
    powder
¼ teaspoon baking soda
1 teaspoon salt
½ cup coarsely chopped
    pecans

Soak apricots in water to cover 5 minutes; drain and coarsely chop. Set aside.

Combine sugar, shortening, and egg in a large mixing bowl; beat well. Gradually add orange juice and water, beating until well blended.

Set aside ¼ cup flour in a small mixing bowl. Sift together remaining flour, baking powder, soda, and salt; gradually add to orange juice mixture, beating well after each addition.

Dredge pecans and reserved apricots in reserved flour. Fold into batter. Spoon batter into a greased 9- x 5- x 3-inch loafpan. Bake at 350° for 1 hour or until a wooden pick inserted in center comes out clean.

Let cool in pan 10 minutes. Remove bread from pan, and cool completely on a wire rack before slicing. Yield: 1 loaf.

"Good bread is the staff of life." Flour ad, c.1890.

Collection of Kit Barry, Brattleboro, Vermont

MISSISSIPPI SPICE MUFFINS

1 cup butter or margarine,
    softened
2 cups sugar
2 eggs
1 (20-ounce) jar unsweetened
    applesauce
1 tablespoon ground
    cinnamon
2 teaspoons ground allspice
1 teaspoon ground cloves
4 cups all-purpose flour
2 teaspoons baking soda
1 teaspoon salt
1 cup pecans, chopped
Sifted powdered sugar

Cream butter in a large mixing bowl; gradually add 2 cups sugar, beating well. Add eggs, one at a time, beating well after each addition. Stir in applesauce and spices, mixing well.

Sift together flour, soda, and salt; add to applesauce mixture, stirring just until dry ingredients are moistened. Fold in pecans.

Spoon batter into greased miniature muffin pans, filling two-thirds full. Bake at 350° for 15 minutes. Remove muffins from pans while still warm; sprinkle with powdered sugar. Serve warm. Yield: 8 dozen.

Note: Batter will keep in refrigerator 1 week.

At any given moment, most of us have the definitive ingredients for hot muffins or quick bread. Berries of any kind, raisins, bananas, nuts, peanut butter . . . just a few possibilities. Quick hot breads are the absolute making of a successful brunch. To ensure a neatly rounded loaf top, let the batter sit in the pan 20 minutes before popping in the oven.

102

OLD-FASHIONED BANANA BREAD

½ cup butter or margarine, softened
1 cup sugar
2 eggs, beaten
2 cups all-purpose flour
½ teaspoon baking soda
⅛ teaspoon salt
1½ cups mashed bananas (3 medium bananas)
½ cup coarsely chopped pecans

Cream butter in a medium mixing bowl; gradually add sugar, beating well. Add eggs, flour, soda, salt, bananas, and pecans; mix well.

Pour batter into a well-greased 9- x 5- x 3-inch loafpan. Bake at 350° for 55 minutes or until a wooden pick inserted in center comes out clean. Cool 10 minutes in pan. Remove bread from pan, and cool completely on a wire rack. Slice and serve. Yield: 1 loaf.

OATMEAL-COCONUT COFFEE CAKE

1½ cups boiling water
1 cup regular oats, uncooked
¼ cup butter or margarine, softened
1 cup firmly packed brown sugar
1 cup sugar
2 eggs, lightly beaten
1⅓ cups all-purpose flour
1 teaspoon baking soda
1 teaspoon salt
1 teaspoon ground cinnamon
1 teaspoon vanilla extract
1 cup flaked coconut
½ cup chopped pecans
½ cup butter or margarine, melted
½ cup firmly packed brown sugar
¼ cup milk
¼ teaspoon vanilla extract

Pour boiling water over oats; let stand 20 minutes.

Cream ¼ cup butter; gradually add 1 cup brown sugar and 1 cup sugar, beating well. Stir in oats mixture. Add next 6 ingredients, and mix well. Spoon mixture into a greased 13- x 9- x 2-inch baking pan. Bake at 350° for 40 minutes or until a wooden pick inserted in center comes out clean.

Combine coconut and pecans; sprinkle mixture over cake. Combine remaining ingredients, and pour over cake. Return cake to oven, and broil 2 minutes or until golden brown. Cut into squares to serve. Yield: 15 to 18 servings.

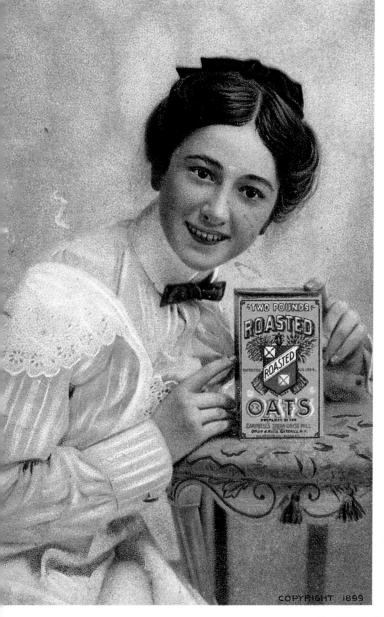

Smiling lady invites attention to Campbell's Steam Grist Mill Roasted Oats. An 1899 trade card.

MORNING COFFEE CAKE

2 cups plus 3 tablespoons
   sugar, divided
¼ cup firmly packed brown
   sugar
3 tablespoons ground
   cinnamon
½ cup chopped pecans
1 cup butter or margarine,
   softened
2 eggs
½ teaspoon vanilla extract
2 cups all-purpose flour
1 teaspoon baking powder
½ teaspoon salt
1 (8-ounce) carton
   commercial sour cream
Cherry Glaze

Combine 3 tablespoons sugar, brown sugar, cinnamon, and pecans in a small mixing bowl; mix well, and set aside.

Cream butter in a large mixing bowl; gradually add remaining 2 cups sugar, beating well. Add eggs, one at a time, beating well after each addition. Stir in vanilla.

Combine flour, baking powder, and salt in a small mixing bowl; add to creamed mixture, mixing well. Fold in sour cream, blending well.

Spoon one-third of batter into a greased and floured 10-inch Bundt pan. Sprinkle half of reserved sugar-cinnamon mixture over batter in pan. Repeat layers with remaining sugar-cinnamon mixture and one-third of batter; spoon remaining batter over top. Swirl with a knife.

Bake at 350° for 1 hour or until a wooden pick inserted comes out clean. Cool in pan 20 minutes. Remove from pan; place on a serving plate. Spoon Cherry Glaze evenly over coffee cake. Slice and serve warm. Yield: one 10-inch coffee cake.

Cherry Glaze:

1 (21-ounce) can cherry pie
   filling
2 to 4 tablespoons Kirsch

Heat pie filling in a medium saucepan, stirring constantly; stir in Kirsch. Yield: 2 cups.

Morning Coffee Cake and squares of Apple Coffee Cake

APPLE COFFEE CAKE

½ cup shortening
1 cup sugar
2 eggs
1 teaspoon vanilla extract
2 cups all-purpose flour
2 teaspoons baking powder
½ teaspoon baking soda
¼ teaspoon salt
1 (8-ounce) carton
   commercial sour cream
1½ cups peeled, chopped
   apple
Topping (recipe follows)

Cream shortening in a medium mixing bowl; gradually add sugar, beating well. Add eggs, one at a time, beating well after each addition. Add vanilla, stirring well.

Combine flour, baking powder, soda, and salt in a small bowl; stir well. Add flour mixture to creamed mixture alternately with sour cream, beginning and ending with flour mixture. Stir in apple.

Spoon batter into a greased 13- x 9- x 3-inch baking pan; sprinkle with topping. Bake at 350° for 35 to 40 minutes. Cut into squares, and serve warm. Yield: 15 to 18 servings.

Topping:

½ cup chopped pecans
½ cup firmly packed brown
   sugar
1 teaspoon ground cinnamon
2 tablespoons butter or
   margarine, melted

Combine all ingredients in a small mixing bowl; stir until crumbly. Yield: about ½ cup.

BLACK COFFEE CAKE

1 cup strong coffee
1 cup water
2 cups firmly packed
  brown sugar
¾ cup butter or margarine,
  softened
4 eggs, separated
4 cups all-purpose flour
1 tablespoon plus 2
  teaspoons baking powder
½ teaspoon salt
2 teaspoons vanilla extract
Crumb Topping

Combine coffee, water, and sugar in a medium saucepan. Bring to a boil, and cook 5 minutes; set aside to cool.

Cream butter in a large mixing bowl. Beat egg yolks until thick and lemon colored; add to butter, mixing well.

Combine flour, baking powder, and salt; sift together 4 times. Add to creamed mixture alternately with coffee mixture, beginning and ending with flour mixture; mix well after each addition. Add vanilla, mixing well.

Beat egg whites (at room temperature) until stiff but not dry; fold into batter.

Pour batter into 2 greased 9-inch round cakepans. Sprinkle liberally with Crumb Topping. Bake at 400° for 30 minutes or until a wooden pick inserted in center comes out clean. Serve warm. Yield: two 9-inch cakes.

Crumb Topping:

1 cup sugar
¾ cup all-purpose flour
¼ teaspoon ground cinnamon
¼ cup plus 2 tablespoons
  butter or margarine,
  softened

Combine all ingredients in a small mixing bowl. Beat at medium speed of an electric mixer until well mixed and crumbly. Yield: about 2 cups.

Metropolitan Life Insurance Company promoted the pasteurization and careful handling of milk to its policy holders, c.1930.

HUCKLEBERRY COFFEE CAKE

½ cup shortening
1 cup sugar
2 eggs, separated
2 cups all-purpose flour
2 teaspoons baking powder
⅛ teaspoon salt
½ teaspoon ground cinnamon
½ teaspoon ground nutmeg
¾ cup plus 2 tablespoons
  milk
2 cups huckleberries or
  blueberries

Cream shortening in a bowl; gradually add sugar, beating well. Beat egg yolks until thick and lemon colored. Add to creamed mixture, mixing well.

Sift together flour, baking powder, salt, cinnamon, and nutmeg. Add to creamed mixture alternately with milk, beginning and ending with flour mixture; stir just until dry ingredients are moistened.

Beat egg whites (at room temperature) until stiff but not dry. Fold egg whites and berries into batter. Spoon into a greased 9-inch square baking pan. Bake at 375° for 45 minutes or until a wooden pick inserted in center comes out clean. Cut into squares, and serve warm. Yield: 9 servings.

SPECIAL YEAST BREADS

ENGLISH MUFFINS

1 cup milk, scalded
¼ cup butter or margarine, divided
2 tablespoons sugar
1 teaspoon salt
4 cups all-purpose flour, divided
1 package dry yeast
¼ cup lukewarm water (105° to 115°)
1 egg, beaten
Cornmeal

Combine milk, 3 tablespoons butter, sugar, and salt in a large mixing bowl; let cool to lukewarm (105° to 115°). Add 2 cups flour, mixing well.

Dissolve yeast in lukewarm water. Let stand 5 minutes. Add dissolved yeast and egg to milk mixture, mixing well. Add remaining flour, mixing well.

Turn dough out onto a lightly floured surface. Knead 1 minute or until dough is smooth and elastic. Place dough in a greased bowl. Melt remaining butter; brush surface of dough lightly with butter. Cover and let rise in a warm place (85°), free from drafts, 1 hour or until doubled in bulk. Punch dough down; cover and let rest 10 minutes.

Turn dough out onto a surface that has been sprinkled with cornmeal. Roll dough to ¼-inch thickness; cut with a 3-inch biscuit cutter. Sprinkle cornmeal over tops of muffins. Place muffins on ungreased baking sheets. Cover and repeat rising procedure 45 minutes or until doubled in bulk.

Place muffins on an ungreased griddle or skillet. Cook over low heat 12 minutes or until browned; turn and cook an additional 12 minutes to brown other side. Split muffins, and toast, if desired. Yield: about 2 dozen.

Brown Brothers

The Universal Bread Maker made kneading easier, c.1915.

QUICK YEAST ROLLS

2 packages dry yeast
2 cups lukewarm milk (105° to 115°)
4½ cups all-purpose flour, divided
3 tablespoons sugar
1 teaspoon salt
1 egg, beaten
¼ cup lard, melted
1 cup butter or margarine, melted

Combine yeast, milk, 1 cup flour, and sugar in a large mixing bowl; stir well. Add 1 cup flour and salt; mix well. Stir in egg and lard. Gradually add remaining flour; stir until well blended. (Dough will be soft.)

Turn dough out onto a floured surface; knead 8 minutes or until smooth and elastic. Roll dough to ¼-inch thickness on a lightly floured surface; cut with a 2-inch biscuit cutter.

Dip each roll in melted butter. Make a crease with a knife across each circle, and fold roll in half. Gently press edges to seal. Place on baking sheets, and let rise in a warm place (85°), free from drafts, 30 minutes or until doubled in bulk. Bake at 400° for 12 minutes or until golden brown. Serve hot. Yield: about 8 dozen.

WHOLE WHEAT ROLLS

2 packages dry yeast
½ cup plus 1 teaspoon sugar, divided
1 cup lukewarm water (105° to 115°)
1 cup boiling water
½ cup shortening
1 teaspoon salt
1 egg, beaten
3 cups all-purpose flour
2 cups whole wheat flour
½ cup butter or margarine, melted
1 cup graham cracker crumbs

Combine yeast, 1 teaspoon sugar, and 1 cup lukewarm water in a small mixing bowl; stir well. Let stand 5 minutes or until bubbly.

Combine 1 cup boiling water, shortening, remaining ½ cup sugar, and salt in a large mixing bowl. Stir until shortening melts and sugar dissolves; let mixture cool to lukewarm (105° to 115°). Stir in yeast mixture and egg, mixing well.

Combine flour in a medium mixing bowl; stir well. Gradually add 2½ cups flour mixture to yeast mixture; beat at low speed of an electric mixer until dough is smooth. Stir in remaining flour mixture to make a soft dough.

Place dough in a greased bowl, turning to grease top. Cover and refrigerate overnight.

Punch dough down. Shape dough with well-greased hands into 1-inch balls; dip each ball in melted butter. Place in lightly greased muffin pans using 3 balls in each muffin cup. Sprinkle graham cracker crumbs evenly over tops of rolls. Cover and let rise in a warm place (85°), free from drafts, 1 hour or until doubled in bulk.

Bake at 375° for 15 minutes or until lightly browned. Serve warm. Yield: 3 dozen.

"Mama used Fleischmann's Yeast" in 1888, according to this trade card. Mamas are still using it today.

REFRIGERATOR ROLLS

2 packages dry yeast
½ cup plus 1 teaspoon sugar, divided
1 cup lukewarm water (105° to 115°)
½ cup shortening
1 teaspoon salt
1 cup boiling water
2 eggs, beaten
6 cups all-purpose flour
Melted butter or margarine

Dissolve yeast and 1 teaspoon sugar in lukewarm water in a small bowl; set aside.

Combine shortening, remaining sugar, salt, and boiling water, stirring until shortening melts. Cool to 105° to 115°. Add yeast mixture and eggs; mix well. Gradually stir in flour to make a soft dough.

Place dough in a well-greased bowl, turning to grease top. Cover and refrigerate overnight.

Punch dough down, and divide into 4 equal portions. Roll each portion into a circle 12 inches in diameter and ¼-inch-thick on a lightly floured surface; cut each circle into 12 wedges. Roll up each wedge tightly, beginning at wide end.

Place rolls on greased baking sheets, point side down; curve into crescent shapes. Brush with melted butter. Cover and let rise in a warm place (85°), free from drafts, 30 minutes or until doubled in bulk. Bake at 400° for 12 minutes or until lightly browned. Serve hot. Yield: 4 dozen.

Collection of Kit Barry, Brattleboro, Vermont

HOT CROSS BUNS

½ cup milk, scalded
¼ cup plus ½ teaspoon sugar, divided
2 tablespoons shortening
¾ teaspoon salt
1 package dry yeast
2 tablespoons lukewarm water (105° to 115°)
1 egg, beaten
2½ cups all-purpose flour, divided
½ teaspoon ground cinnamon
½ cup raisins
½ cup sifted powdered sugar
2 teaspoons milk

Combine scalded milk, ¼ cup sugar, shortening, and salt; let cool to lukewarm (105° to 115°). Dissolve yeast and remaining ½ teaspoon sugar in lukewarm water in a large mixing bowl, stirring well. Let stand 5 minutes or until bubbly.

Add milk mixture and egg to yeast mixture. Add 1 cup flour, mixing until smooth. Combine remaining flour, cinnamon, and raisins in a small mixing bowl, stirring well to dredge; add cinnamon mixture to yeast mixture, stirring to make a soft dough.

Turn dough out onto a lightly floured surface. Knead 8 minutes or until smooth and elastic. Place dough in a greased bowl, turning to grease top. Cover and let rise in a warm place (85°), free from drafts, 1½ hours or until doubled in bulk. Punch dough down. Turn out onto a lightly floured surface. Cover and let rest 10 minutes.

Divide dough into 9 pieces; shape into balls, and place ½ inch apart in a greased 9-inch square baking pan. Cover and repeat rising procedure 1 hour or until doubled in bulk.

Bake at 425° for 20 minutes or until golden brown; cool slightly.

Combine powdered sugar and 2 teaspoons milk in a small mixing bowl; stir until smooth. Pipe icing into cross shape on each bun. Yield: 1½ dozen.

Hot Cross Buns are an Easter-time special treat.

ORANGE ROLLS

1 package dry yeast
¼ cup sugar, divided
2 tablespoons lukewarm water (105° to 115°)
1 cup boiling water
2 tablespoons shortening
1 teaspoon salt
4 to 4½ cups all-purpose flour, divided
1 egg, beaten
2 cups orange marmalade
Glaze (recipes follows)

Dissolve yeast and 1 teaspoon sugar in lukewarm water; stir well. Let stand 5 minutes or until bubbly.

Combine boiling water, shortening, remaining sugar, and salt in a large mixing bowl. Stir in 2 cups flour and egg, beating well. Stir in yeast mixture, and add enough remaining flour to make a soft dough. Turn dough out onto a floured surface, and knead 8 minutes or until smooth and elastic.

Place dough in a greased bowl, turning to grease top. Cover and let rise in a warm place (85°), free from drafts, 1 hour or until doubled in bulk.

Punch dough down, and let rest 5 minutes. Divide dough in half. Roll each half into an 18- x 10-inch rectangle on a lightly floured surface. Spread 1 cup orange marmalade over each dough rectangle, leaving a ½-inch margin. Roll up jellyroll fashion, starting at long side. Cut roll into 1-inch slices. Place slices, cut side down, in greased muffin pans.

Cover and repeat rising procedure 45 minutes or until doubled in bulk. Bake at 375° for 15 minutes or until rolls are browned. Remove rolls from pans immediately. Pour glaze over warm rolls, and serve. Yield: about 3 dozen.

Glaze:

2 cups sifted powdered sugar
3 to 4 tablespoons orange juice

Combine sugar and orange juice, mixing well. Use immediately. Yield: about ¾ cup.

The Open Air Breakfast, *an oil on canvas by William Merritt Chase, c.1888.*

EVERLASTING BREAD

1 package dry yeast
½ cup plus 1 teaspoon sugar, divided
½ cup lukewarm water (105° to 115°)
4 cups milk, scalded and cooled to lukewarm (105° to 115°)
1 cup vegetable oil
2 teaspoons baking powder
1 tablespoon plus 2 teaspoons salt
11 cups all-purpose flour, divided

Dissolve yeast and 1 teaspoon sugar in water, stirring well; let stand 5 minutes.

Combine yeast, remaining sugar, milk, oil, baking powder, and salt in a large mixing bowl; mix well. Stir in 2 cups flour. Cover; let rise in a warm place (85°), free from drafts, 1 hour or until doubled in bulk.

Stir dough mixture; add enough remaining flour to make a stiff dough. Turn dough out onto a heavily floured surface; knead 8 minutes or until smooth and elastic.

Place in a large, well-greased bowl, turning to grease top.

Cover and refrigerate overnight.

Divide dough into three equal portions; shape each into a loaf. Place in 3 greased 9- x 5- x 3-inch loafpans. Cover and repeat rising procedure 1½ hours or until doubled in bulk.

Bake at 350° for 50 minutes or until loaves sound hollow when tapped. Remove bread from pans immediately; cool on wire racks. Slice and serve. Yield: 3 loaves.

Note: All or portions of the dough may be kept covered and refrigerated 4 to 5 days.

RAISIN BREAD

3½ to 3¾ cups all-purpose
　flour, divided
¼ cup sugar
1½ teaspoons salt
2 packages dry yeast
½ cup milk
½ cup water
¼ cup butter or margarine
2 eggs
1 teaspoon vanilla extract
3 cups raisins
2 tablespoons butter or
　margarine, melted
Glaze (recipe follows)

Combine 1¼ cups flour, sugar, salt, and yeast in a large bowl. Heat milk, water, and ¼ cup butter in a saucepan to 120° to 130°. Add to dry ingredients; beat 2 minutes at medium speed of an electric mixer, scraping bowl often. Add eggs, one at a time, beating well after each addition. Add ¾ cup flour and vanilla; beat 2 minutes at high speed. Dredge raisins in ¼ cup flour; stir into dough. Add enough remaining flour to make a soft dough.

Turn dough out onto a lightly floured surface; knead 5 minutes or until smooth and elastic. Place in a greased bowl, turning to grease top. Cover; let rise in a warm place (85°), free from drafts, 1½ hours or until doubled in bulk. Punch dough down; let rest 15 minutes.

Divide dough in half; shape each half into a loaf. Place in 2 greased 8½- x 4½- x 3-inch loafpans. Cover and repeat rising procedure 30 minutes or until doubled in bulk.

Bake at 375° for 25 minutes or until loaves sound hollow when tapped. Cool in pans 10 minutes; transfer bread to wire racks. Brush with butter; drizzle glaze over top. Slice when cool. Yield: 2 loaves.

Glaze:

1 cup sifted powdered sugar
1½ tablespoons milk
¼ teaspoon almond extract

Combine all ingredients in a small bowl; mix well. Use immediately. Yield: about ½ cup.

BRAIDED COFFEE CAKE

2 packages dry yeast
2 cups sugar, divided
1 cup lukewarm water (105°
　to 115°)
1 cup butter or margarine
1½ teaspoons salt
1 cup boiling water
2 eggs, lightly beaten
8 cups all-purpose flour,
　divided
¾ cup butter or margarine,
　melted
1½ cups firmly packed
　brown sugar
½ cup finely chopped pecans
1 tablespoon ground
　cinnamon
Additional melted butter or
　margarine
Glaze (recipe follows)

Dissolve yeast and 1 teaspoon sugar in lukewarm water; let stand 5 minutes or until mixture is bubbly.

Place 1 cup butter, salt, and ½ cup sugar in a large mixing bowl; add boiling water, stirring until butter melts. Add yeast mixture and eggs, stirring until well blended. Stir in enough flour to form a stiff dough. Cover and refrigerate overnight.

Turn dough out onto a lightly floured surface, and divide into 3 equal portions. Divide each portion into 3 equal pieces. Roll each piece into a 25- x 10-inch rectangle. On each rectangle, brush half of long side evenly with ¾ cup melted butter. Combine remaining sugar, brown sugar, chopped pecans, and cinnamon; sprinkle mixture evenly over melted butter.

Roll each rectangle up jellyroll fashion, beginning at long side; moisten edges with water to seal. Braid ropes, pinching edges to seal. Place each braided loaf in a greased 9- x 5- x 3-inch loafpan; brush with additional melted butter.

Let loaves rise in a warm place (85°), free from drafts, 45 minutes or until doubled in bulk. Bake at 350° for 35 minutes or until loaves sound hollow when tapped. Remove bread from pans immediately; cool on wire racks. Drizzle glaze over tops of warm loaves. Slice and serve warm. Yield: 3 loaves.

Glaze:

3 cups sifted powdered sugar
¼ cup plus 2 tablespoons
　milk
1½ teaspoons vanilla extract

Combine all ingredients, mixing well. Use immediately. Yield: 1½ cups.

Swirl Coffee Cake:

For swirl coffee cake variation, divide dough into 3 equal portions. Roll each portion into a 25- x 10-inch rectangle; brush with melted butter. Sprinkle cinnamon mixture evenly over each rectangle of dough. Roll up jellyroll fashion, beginning at long side; moisten edges with water to seal.

Shape each rope into a loose coil in 3 greased 9-inch round cakepans, beginning at outer edge of pan. Sprinkle with additional cinnamon and sugar, if desired. Repeat rising procedure 45 minutes or until doubled in bulk. Bake at 350° for 30 minutes or until golden brown. Remove from pans; drizzle glaze over coffee cake. Slice and serve warm. Yield: three 9-inch cakes.

TOASTED, GRIDDLED, AND FRIED

Cover for a booklet on toast, c.1926.

CINNAMON GLAZED TOAST

6 slices bread
1 tablespoon butter or
  margarine, softened
½ cup sifted powdered sugar
1 tablespoon whipping cream
½ teaspoon ground cinnamon

Remove crust from bread; cut each slice in half lengthwise. Toast bread.

Cream butter in a small mixing bowl; add sugar, whipping cream, and cinnamon, beating well. Spread mixture evenly over one side of toasted bread. Broil 3 to 4 inches from heating element until bubbly and lightly browned. Serve immediately. Yield: 6 servings.

ORANGE-CINNAMON TOAST

½ cup firmly packed brown sugar
1 tablespoon grated orange rind
¼ cup orange juice
1 teaspoon ground cinnamon
8 slices bread
3 tablespoons butter or margarine, softened

Combine sugar, orange rind, juice, and cinnamon in a small saucepan; bring to a boil. Reduce heat, and simmer 8 minutes or until syrupy.

Spread one side of each bread slice with butter; place bread, buttered side up, on baking sheet. Spread 1 tablespoon sugar mixture over each slice.

Broil 4 inches from heating element until browned. Serve immediately. Yield: 4 servings.

FRENCH TOAST

1 cup milk
4 eggs
¼ teaspoon salt
⅛ teaspoon pepper
2 tablespoons butter
8 slices bread
Additional butter
Maple syrup

Combine milk, eggs, salt, and pepper in a shallow bowl, beating well.

Melt 2 tablespoons butter in a large skillet; dip 2 bread slices, one at a time, into egg mixture, coating well. Drain; arrange in skillet, and cook over medium heat 4 minutes on each side or until lightly browned. Remove to a serving platter; keep warm. Repeat with remaining bread slices, adding butter to skillet as needed. Serve warm with syrup. Yield: 4 servings.

ORANGE FRENCH TOAST

3 eggs, well beaten
¼ cup sifted powdered sugar
1 teaspoon ground cinnamon
2 teaspoons grated orange rind
⅔ cup orange juice
¼ cup plus 2 tablespoons butter or margarine, divided
12 slices bread
Additional sifted powdered sugar

Combine eggs, ¼ cup powdered sugar, cinnamon, orange rind, and juice in a shallow pan; stir well.

Melt 1 tablespoon butter in a large skillet over medium heat; dip 2 bread slices, one at a time, into egg mixture, coating well. Let drain; arrange in skillet, and cook 4 minutes on each side or until browned. Remove to a serving platter; keep warm. Sprinkle with powdered sugar.

Repeat procedure with remaining bread slices. Serve warm. Yield: 6 servings.

Toast and tea are a welcome treat at any time of day.

Pain Perdu is a practical Creole solution to bread going stale; it turns a liability into an asset.

PAIN PERDU

2 cups milk
1 cup sugar, divided
2 tablespoons brandy or 1 teaspoon vanilla extract
12 slices bread, crust removed
5 eggs, separated
1 tablespoon grated lemon rind
¼ cup butter or margarine, divided
2 tablespoons lard, divided
¼ teaspoon ground cinnamon

Bring milk to a boil in a small saucepan. Remove from heat. Stir in ½ cup sugar and brandy.

Place bread slices in a single layer in a 15- x 10- x 1-inch jellyroll pan. Pour milk mixture over bread, and let stand 10 minutes. Drain off excess milk.

Beat egg yolks until thick and lemon colored. Add 2 tablespoons sugar and lemon rind, beating well. Beat egg whites (at room temperature) until soft peaks form. Gradually add 2 tablespoons sugar, beating until stiff peaks form. Fold into egg yolk mixture. Spread egg mixture evenly over bread; let stand 30 minutes.

Melt 2 tablespoons butter and 1 tablespoon lard in a large skillet over medium-high heat. Lift bread slices, one at a time, with a spatula, and place in hot butter mixture. Cook 2 to 3 at a time until golden brown, turning once. Remove to a platter, and keep warm. Repeat procedure with remaining bread slices, adding butter and lard as needed.

Combine remaining ¼ cup sugar and cinnamon; sprinkle over bread slices. Serve warm. Yield: 6 servings.

BUTTERMILK PANCAKES

1¾ cups all-purpose flour
2 teaspoons sugar
1½ teaspoons baking powder
1 teaspoon baking soda
1 teaspoon salt
2 cups buttermilk
2 eggs, beaten
¼ cup butter or margarine, melted

Combine flour, sugar, baking powder, soda, and salt in a medium mixing bowl. Combine buttermilk and eggs; slowly stir into dry ingredients. Add butter, mixing lightly. (Batter will be lumpy.)

For each pancake, pour ¼ cup batter onto a hot, lightly greased griddle or skillet. Cook until tops of pancakes are covered with bubbles and edges appear slightly dry. Turn and cook until bottom sides are browned. Serve immediately. Yield: eighteen 4-inch pancakes.

COTTAGE CHEESE PANCAKES

½ cup wheat germ
4 eggs
1 (8-ounce) carton cream-style cottage cheese
1 tablespoon vegetable oil
1 tablespoon honey
1 teaspoon vanilla extract
Dash of salt

Combine all ingredients in container of an electric blender; process until smooth.

For each pancake, pour ¼ cup batter onto a hot, lightly greased griddle or skillet. Cook until tops of pancakes are covered with bubbles and edges appear slightly dry. Turn and continue cooking until bottom sides are browned. Serve immediately. Yield: twelve 4-inch pancakes.

ALSATIAN PANCAKE

¼ cup plus 2 tablespoons
   butter or margarine
½ cup all-purpose flour
½ cup milk
2 eggs, lightly beaten
¼ teaspoon ground nutmeg
½ cup sifted powdered sugar
Red Plum Jelly (page 11)

Place butter in a 10-inch pie-plate; bake at 425° until butter melts. Remove from oven, and set aside.

Combine flour, milk, eggs, and nutmeg in a medium mixing bowl; stir until well blended. Pour flour mixture into butter (do not stir). Bake at 425° for 15 minutes; remove from oven, and sprinkle with powdered sugar. Bake an additional 5 minutes. Cool slightly; cut into wedges. Serve with Red Plum Jelly. Yield: 4 to 6 servings.

APPLE-RICE GRIDDLE CAKES

1 cup all-purpose flour
1 tablespoon sugar
1 tablespoon baking powder
½ teaspoon salt
½ teaspoon ground cinnamon
¼ teaspoon ground nutmeg
¾ cup milk
2 eggs, lightly beaten
2 tablespoons shortening,
   melted
1 cup cooked regular rice
1 apple, peeled and grated
½ cup chopped pecans,
   toasted

Sift first 6 ingredients into a medium bowl. Combine milk, eggs, and shortening; stir into dry mixture. Fold in remaining ingredients.

For each griddle cake, pour ¼ cup batter onto a hot, lightly greased griddle. Cook until tops are covered with bubbles and edges appear slightly dry. Turn and continue cooking until bottom sides are browned. Serve warm. Yield: twelve 4-inch griddle cakes.

BASIC WAFFLES

2 eggs, beaten
1¼ cups milk
¼ cup plus 2 tablespoons
   vegetable oil
2 cups all-purpose flour
1 tablespoon baking powder
1 teaspoon salt

Combine eggs, milk, and oil in a medium bowl; mix well.

Sift together flour, baking powder, and salt; add to egg mixture, stirring well.

Spoon batter into a pre-heated, lightly oiled waffle iron, following manufacturer's directions. Cook 5 minutes or until brown and crisp. Remove waffle; keep warm. Repeat procedure with remaining batter. Serve hot with butter and syrup. Yield: eight 4-inch waffles.

Cheese Waffles:

For cheese waffles, add ½ cup (2 ounces) shredded Cheddar cheese to batter before baking.

Ham Waffles:

For ham waffles, sprinkle 1 tablespoon finely chopped cooked ham over batter of each waffle before closing waffle iron.

CRISPY WAFFLES

2 cups all-purpose flour
2 teaspoons baking powder
½ teaspoon salt
1¼ cups milk
3 eggs, separated
¼ cup butter or margarine,
   melted

Combine first 3 ingredients in a medium bowl; mix well. Add milk, egg yolks, and butter; stir until smooth.

Beat egg whites (at room temperature) in a small bowl until stiff; gently fold into batter.

Spoon batter into a pre-heated, lightly oiled waffle iron, following manufacturer's directions. Cook 5 minutes or until brown and crisp. Repeat procedure with remaining batter. Yield: ten 4-inch waffles.

Appealing child portrays Grandma on this trade card, c.1890.

"Buglin' Sam" Dekemel and his father made and sold genuine hot waffles from this wagon. New Orleans, c.1920.

WHOLE WHEAT WAFFLES

1 cup all-purpose flour
1 cup whole wheat flour
1 tablespoon sugar
2 teaspoons baking powder
1 teaspoon baking soda
½ teaspoon salt
2 cups buttermilk
3 eggs, beaten
½ cup shortening, melted

Combine first 6 ingredients in a large bowl; mix well. Add remaining ingredients; beat until smooth.

Spoon batter into a preheated, lightly oiled waffle iron, following manufacturer's directions. Cook 5 minutes or until brown and crisp. Repeat procedure with remaining batter. Yield: twelve 4-inch waffles.

CORN WAFFLES

1½ cups white cornmeal
¾ cup bread flour
1 tablespoon baking powder
½ teaspoon baking soda
2 tablespoons sugar
1 teaspoon salt
2 eggs, separated
1½ cups buttermilk
¼ cup shortening, melted

Combine first 6 ingredients; sift together 3 times.

Beat egg yolks until thick and lemon colored; add dry ingredients alternately with buttermilk, beginning and ending with dry ingredients. Mix well.

Beat egg whites (at room temperature) until stiff but not dry. Fold egg whites and melted shortening into egg yolk mixture. Spoon batter into a preheated, lightly oiled waffle iron, following manufacturer's directions. Cook 5 minutes or until waffle is brown and crisp. Repeat procedure with remaining batter. Serve warm. Yield: eight 4-inch waffles.

GINGERBREAD WAFFLES

½ cup butter or margarine
½ cup sugar
2 eggs, beaten
¾ cup molasses
2 cups all-purpose flour
1½ teaspoons baking soda
½ teaspoon salt
2 teaspoons ground ginger
1 teaspoon ground cinnamon
¼ teaspoon ground cloves
1 cup boiling water

Cream butter; gradually add sugar, beating until light and fluffy. Add eggs and molasses, beating until smooth.

Sift together dry ingredients; add to creamed mixture alternately with water, beginning and ending with dry ingredients; stir well.

Spoon batter into a preheated, lightly oiled waffle iron, following manufacturer's directions. Cook 5 minutes or until brown and crisp. Repeat procedure with remaining batter. Yield: twelve 4-inch waffles.

SWEET POTATO WAFFLES

1¼ cups milk
1 cup cooked, mashed sweet potatoes
¼ cup butter or margarine, melted
2 eggs, lightly beaten
2 cups all-purpose flour
3 tablespoons sugar

Combine milk, sweet potatoes, butter, and eggs in a medium bowl; mix well. Combine flour and sugar; add to milk mixture, stirring well.

Spoon batter into a preheated, lightly oiled waffle iron, following manufacturer's directions. Cook 5 minutes or until brown and crisp. Repeat procedure with remaining batter. Yield: ten 4-inch waffles.

PINEAPPLE FRITTERS

1 cup all-purpose flour
1 tablespoon sugar
1 teaspoon baking powder
¼ teaspoon salt
2 eggs, separated
⅓ cup milk
1 tablespoon butter or margarine, melted
1 (8-ounce) can pineapple tidbits, drained
Vegetable oil
¼ cup sugar
¼ teaspoon ground cinnamon

Combine flour, 1 tablespoon sugar, baking powder, and salt in a medium mixing bowl; stir well. Beat egg yolks in a small mixing bowl. Add milk, beating well. Stir milk mixture into dry ingredients; add melted butter, stirring just until moistened.

Beat egg whites (at room temperature) until stiff peaks form. Fold into flour mixture. Gently stir in pineapple.

Drop mixture by tablespoonfuls into deep, hot oil (375°). Fry until golden brown, turning once. Drain on paper towels.

Combine ¼ cup sugar and cinnamon in a small mixing bowl. Roll fritters in sugar mixture. Serve immediately. Yield: about 2 dozen.

CRULLERS

¼ cup shortening
1 cup sugar
2 eggs, beaten
4¼ cups all-purpose flour
1 tablespoon baking powder
½ teaspoon salt
½ teaspoon ground nutmeg
1 cup milk
Vegetable oil
Sifted powdered sugar

Cream shortening in a large mixing bowl; gradually add sugar, beating well. Add eggs; beat well.

Sift together flour, baking powder, salt, and nutmeg; add to creamed mixture alternately with milk, beginning and ending with flour mixture. (Dough will be soft.) Chill 1 hour.

Turn dough out onto a heavily floured surface; dust dough heavily with flour. Knead 4 to 5 times; roll dough to ¼-inch thickness. Cut into 9- x ¾-inch strips; fold each strip in half. Twist folded strip; press ends together to seal.

Heat 3 to 4 inches oil to 375°; gently drop in 3 to 4 crullers at a time. Cook 1 minute or until golden brown on one side; turn and cook 1 minute on other side. Drain on paper towels; sprinkle with powdered sugar. Repeat procedure with remaining dough. Serve warm. Yield: about 3 dozen.

Brown Brothers

An irresistible smile goes with an irresistible product: A waffle iron demonstration in the 1920s.

BANANA PUFFS

2 eggs, separated
¾ cup mashed banana (about 2 medium bananas)
1 tablespoon butter or margarine, melted
⅓ cup milk
1½ cups all-purpose flour
1 teaspoon baking powder
Vegetable oil
Sifted powdered sugar

Beat egg yolks in a medium mixing bowl until light and lemon colored. Add mashed banana, butter, and milk, stirring mixture well.

Sift together flour and baking powder. Add to banana mixture, mixing well.

Beat egg whites (at room temperature) in a small mixing bowl until stiff, but not dry; fold into batter.

Drop batter by teaspoonfuls into deep, hot oil (375°). Fry until golden brown, turning once. Drain well on paper towels. Dredge in powdered sugar. Serve warm. Yield: about 4 dozen.

FREDERICKSBURG ORANGE DOUGHNUTS

¼ cup butter or margarine, softened
1 cup sugar
2 eggs
1 tablespoon grated orange rind
3 tablespoons orange juice
5 cups all-purpose flour
1 tablespoon baking powder
1 teaspoon salt
1 cup milk
Lard or shortening
Additional sugar

Cream butter in a large mixing bowl; gradually add 1 cup sugar, beating well. Add eggs, rind, and juice; beat well.

Sift together flour, baking powder, and salt; add to creamed mixture alternately with milk, beginning and ending with flour mixture.

Place dough on a floured surface; roll to ¼-inch thickness. Cut dough with a floured doughnut cutter.

Drop doughnuts 3 to 4 at a time into deep, hot oil (375°). Cook 1 minute or until golden brown on one side; turn and cook 1 minute on other side. Drain well. Roll doughnuts in additional sugar; serve warm. Yield: about 1½ dozen.

Deep-fried pastries are the siren song the dieter tries to ignore. But there are times when we feel they're imperative to our well-being. Freshness and temperature of the cooking oil are most important for flavor and digestibility. A temperature of 375° ensures that the pastries will not absorb too much oil. Test for doneness: break open the first piece to see if it is cooked through. Always drain thoroughly and serve them as hot as possible.

FAVORITE EGG AND CHEESE DISHES

Farm woman has made a successful raid on her chicken coop in this photograph taken c.1915.

BAKED EGGS

8 eggs
Salt and pepper to taste
¼ cup half-and-half, divided
1 tablespoon plus 1 teaspoon
  butter or margarine, divided

Break 2 eggs, and gently slip into a greased 10-ounce custard cup or ramekin. Sprinkle eggs with salt and pepper to taste. Top with 1 tablespoon half-and-half and 1 teaspoon butter. Repeat procedure with remaining ingredients.

Bake at 350° for 15 minutes or until whites are set and yolks are soft and creamy. Serve immediately. Yield: 4 servings.

Note: This is a good way to prepare eggs in quantity.

POACHED EGGS

3 cups water
4 eggs

Lightly oil a 1½-quart saucepan; add water, and bring to a boil over medium-high heat. Reduce heat to keep water at a simmer.

Carefully break eggs, one at a time, into a small saucer; gently slip each egg into water, holding dish close to surface of water. Simmer, uncovered, 2 to 3 minutes depending on desired degree of doneness. Remove eggs with a slotted spoon, and drain on paper towels; trim edges, if desired. Serve immediately. Yield: 2 servings.

SOFT-COOKED EGGS

4 eggs

Place eggs in a medium saucepan. Cover with water one inch above eggs. Cover and cook over high heat, bringing water to a boil. Remove from heat; leave eggs, covered, in hot water for 1 to 4 minutes, depending on desired degree of doneness.

Remove eggs from pan with a slotted spoon; place eggs in a bowl of ice water until cool enough to handle.

To serve, break shell at widest point with knife. Scoop egg out of shell, and serve immediately. Yield: 4 servings.

SCRAMBLED EGGS WITH MUSHROOMS AND ONIONS

2 tablespoons chopped onion
3 tablespoons butter or
  margarine
3 eggs, beaten
¼ teaspoon salt
¼ teaspoon pepper
½ cup (2 ounces) cubed
  Cheddar cheese
1 (3-ounce) can sliced
  mushrooms, drained
2 tablespoons canned green
  peas, drained (optional)
Chopped fresh parsley

Sauté onion in butter in a medium skillet over medium heat until tender.

Combine eggs, salt, pepper, cheese, mushrooms, and peas, if desired, in a small mixing bowl; stir gently, and add to onion in skillet. Cook, stirring frequently, until eggs are set but still moist and cheese begins to melt. Transfer egg mixture to a warm serving plate; sprinkle with parsley. Serve immediately. Yield: 2 to 4 servings.

This restaurant machine for boiling eggs featured variable timers. Operator did have to remember who ordered the 3-minute egg.

SCRAMBLED EGGS AND RICE

6 eggs
1 cup cooked regular rice
½ cup chopped green onion
½ cup chopped green pepper
¼ cup milk
1 tablespoon chopped fresh
  parsley
½ teaspoon salt
¼ teaspoon pepper
¼ cup butter or margarine
¾ cup (3 ounces) shredded
  process American cheese
Red sweet pepper rings

Beat eggs with a fork until blended; stir in rice, onion, green pepper, milk, parsley, salt, and pepper.

Melt butter in a large skillet; add egg mixture. Cook over low heat, stirring often, until eggs are firm but still moist. Spoon onto a serving platter; sprinkle with cheese. Garnish with pepper rings. Yield: 4 servings.

BURRITOS DE HUEVOS CON CHORIZO

8 flour tortillas
1 pound Chorizo sausage
  (page 37)
4 eggs, beaten
Commercial taco sauce

Wrap tortillas tightly in aluminum foil; bake at 350° for 15 minutes.

Crumble sausage in a large skillet; cook over medium heat until browned. Drain off pan drippings.

Stir eggs into sausage. Cook over medium heat, stirring constantly, until eggs are set.

Spoon ¼ cup sausage mixture just off center of each tortilla. Fold edge nearest meat filling up and over filling, just until mixture is covered. Fold in sides to center; roll up. Repeat with remaining ingredients. Serve with taco sauce. Yield: 8 burritos.

Museum of the City of New York

FLUFFY HAM OMELET

4 eggs, separated
¼ cup water
⅛ teaspoon salt
⅛ teaspoon pepper
2 tablespoons butter or
    margarine
¾ cup chopped cooked ham
Fresh parsley sprigs

Beat egg yolks in a medium mixing bowl until thick and lemon colored; add water, salt, and pepper, mixing well.

Beat egg whites (at room temperature) in a small mixing bowl until stiff but not dry; fold into yolk mixture.

Heat an ovenproof 10-inch omelet pan or heavy skillet over medium heat until hot enough to sizzle a drop of water. Add butter, rotating pan to coat bottom and sides. Pour in egg mixture, and gently smooth surface. Reduce heat; cook 5 minutes or until puffy and lightly browned on the bottom. Transfer pan to oven; bake, uncovered, at 350° for 7 minutes or until a knife inserted in center comes out clean.

Sprinkle chopped ham over half of omelet. Loosen omelet with spatula, and fold in half. Gently slide omelet onto a warm serving plate. Garnish with parsley. Serve immediately. Yield: 2 servings.

FRESH HERB OMELET

6 eggs, lightly beaten
¼ cup plus 2 tablespoons
    milk
1 tablespoon butter or
    margarine
½ teaspoon salt
1 teaspoon chopped fresh
    parsley
1 teaspoon chopped fresh
    chives
1 teaspoon chopped fresh
    marjoram
1 teaspoon chopped fresh
    rosemary

Combine eggs and milk in a small mixing bowl; mix just until blended. Heat butter in a 10-inch omelet pan or heavy skillet over medium heat.

Pour egg mixture into skillet all at once. As mixture starts to cook, gently lift edges of omelet with a spatula; tilt pan to allow uncooked portion to flow underneath. Cook until set but not dry. Sprinkle with salt.

Combine parsley, chives, marjoram, and rosemary; sprinkle over half the omelet, reserving 1 teaspoon herbs. Fold opposite side of omelet over herbs; transfer to a warm serving platter. Garnish with reserved herbs, and serve immediately. Yield: 2 to 4 servings.

CHEESE OMELET

6 eggs, separated
1 cup (4 ounces) shredded
  Cheddar cheese
⅓ cup soft breadcrumbs
2 tablespoons chopped fresh
  parsley
Salt and pepper to taste
2 tablespoons butter or
  margarine

Beat egg yolks until thick and lemon colored. Add cheese, breadcrumbs, parsley, and salt and pepper; stir well. Beat egg whites (at room temperature) until stiff but not dry; fold into yolk mixture.

Melt butter in a large ovenproof skillet over medium heat. Pour in egg mixture; gently smooth surface. Cook 5 minutes or until bottom is lightly browned. Transfer omelet pan to oven; bake, uncovered, at 350° for 8 minutes or until a knife inserted in center comes out clean. Fold omelet in half; transfer to a warm serving plate. Yield: 4 servings.

CORN OMELET

4 ears fresh corn
½ cup half-and-half
½ teaspoon salt
Dash of pepper
4 eggs, separated
2 tablespoons butter or
  margarine

Cut corn from cob, scraping cob to remove pulp. Combine corn, half-and-half, salt, and pepper in a large mixing bowl. Beat egg yolks until thick and lemon colored; stir into corn mixture.

Beat egg whites (at room temperature) until stiff peaks form; fold into corn mixture.

Melt butter in a large ovenproof skillet over low heat; add egg mixture. Cook over low heat 20 minutes. Transfer omelet pan to oven, and bake at 350° for 10 minutes or until set. Remove from oven; fold omelet in half. Slide onto a warm serving plate. Serve immediately. Yield: 2 to 4 servings.

SOUR CREAM OMELET

5 eggs, separated
1 (8-ounce) carton
  commercial sour cream,
  divided
½ teaspoon salt
2 tablespoons butter or
  margarine
Fresh whole strawberries

Beat egg whites (at room temperature) until stiff but not dry; set aside. Beat egg yolks in a medium mixing bowl until thick and lemon colored. Stir ½ cup sour cream and salt into yolks; fold whites into yolk mixture.

Melt butter in an ovenproof 10-inch omelet pan or heavy skillet; rotate pan to coat bottom. Pour in egg mixture all at once; gently smooth surface. Cook over low heat 20 minutes or until puffy and lightly browned on bottom, gently lifting omelet to judge color. Transfer pan to oven, and bake at 350° for 5 minutes or until a knife inserted in center comes out clean.

Slide omelet onto a warm serving plate; cut into wedges. Top with remaining sour cream and strawberries, and serve. Yield: 4 servings.

NEW FAMILY STRAWBERRY "HILTON GEM"

EGGS SARDOU

½ pound fresh spinach,
  cleaned
3 tablespoons whipping
  cream
¼ teaspoon salt
1 (14-ounce) can artichoke
  bottoms, heated and
  drained
6 poached eggs
Hollandaise Sauce (see next
  recipe)

Place spinach in a Dutch oven (do not add water); cover and cook over high heat 8 to 10 minutes. Drain well.

Combine spinach, whipping cream, and salt in container of an electric blender; process until smooth.

Place creamed spinach mixture into 6 heated artichoke bottoms. Place 1 poached egg on top of each bed of spinach; arrange on individual serving plates. Cover each with Hollandaise Sauce; serve immediately. Yield: 6 servings.

WEIDMANN'S EGGS BENEDICT

3 English muffins, halved
6 slices fully-cooked ham
6 thick slices tomato
6 poached eggs
Hollandaise Sauce
6 green pepper rings
Paprika

Toast muffin halves until lightly browned. Place ham and tomato slices on grill 4 inches from medium coals; grill 3 minutes on each side.

Place 1 ham slice and 1 tomato slice on each muffin half. Top each with a poached egg, and cover with Hollandaise Sauce. Garnish with green pepper rings; sprinkle with paprika. Serve immediately. Yield: 6 servings.

Hollandaise Sauce:

4 egg yolks
2 tablespoons lemon juice
1 cup butter or margarine,
  softened and divided
¼ teaspoon salt
Dash of red pepper

Combine egg yolks and lemon juice in top of a double boiler; beat with a wire whisk until blended. Add ⅓ cup butter. Bring water to a boil (water in bottom of double boiler should not touch pan). Reduce heat to low; cook, stirring constantly, until butter melts. Add ⅓ cup butter; stir constantly until butter begins to melt. Add remaining butter, stirring constantly, until melted. Cook, stirring constantly, 2 minutes or until smooth and thickened. Remove from heat; stir in salt and pepper. Yield: about 1 cup.

Weidmann's Eggs Benedict with real Hollandaise Sauce is a choice main dish for breakfast or brunch.

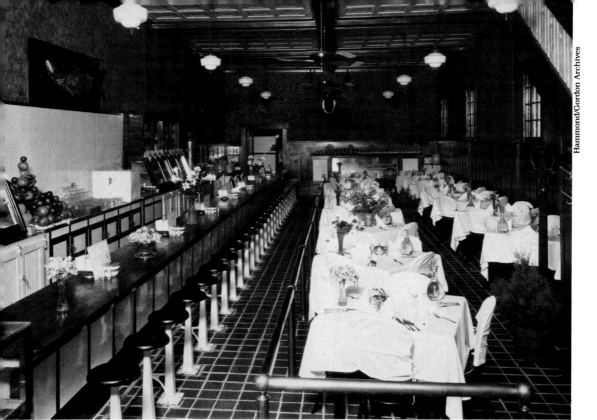

Interior of Weidmann's Restaurant in Meridian, Mississippi. Photo c.1926.

Hammond/Gordon Archives

TOMATO EGGS

¼ cup tomato puree, divided
4 poached eggs
1 tablespoon butter or
  margarine
1 tablespoon all-purpose flour
½ cup milk
½ cup (2 ounces) shredded
  sharp Cheddar cheese
Salt and pepper to taste

Place 1 tablespoon tomato puree in four 6-ounce custard cups. Place one poached egg on top of puree in each cup. Set cups aside.

Melt butter in a small saucepan over low heat; add flour, stirring until smooth. Cook 1 minute, stirring constantly. Gradually add milk; cook over medium heat, stirring constantly, until thickened and bubbly.

Spoon equal amounts of white sauce over eggs in custard cups. Sprinkle cheese over top of white sauce; add salt and pepper. Bake at 350° for 5 minutes or until cheese melts. Serve immediately. Yield: 4 servings.

BAKED CREOLE EGG CASSEROLE

1 large onion, chopped
1 large green pepper, chopped
3 stalks celery, chopped
¼ cup plus 1 tablespoon
  butter or margarine, divided
1 (14½-ounce) can whole
  tomatoes, undrained
¾ teaspoon salt, divided
½ teaspoon pepper
Red pepper to taste
¼ cup all-purpose flour
1 cup milk
1 tablespoon Worcestershire
  sauce
10 hard-cooked eggs, thinly
  sliced
1 cup soft breadcrumbs
2 tablespoons butter or
  margarine, melted

Sauté onion, green pepper, and celery in 2 tablespoons butter in a large skillet until tender. Stir in tomatoes, ½ teaspoon salt, and pepper. Bring to a boil; reduce heat. Cover and simmer 20 minutes or until mixture is thickened, stirring occasionally. Remove from heat, and set aside.

Melt 3 tablespoons butter in a large saucepan over low heat; add flour, stirring until smooth. Cook 1 minute, stirring constantly. Gradually add milk; cook over medium heat, stirring constantly, until thickened and bubbly. Add Worcestershire sauce and remaining salt; stir well. Stir in vegetables and eggs. Spoon into a lightly greased 2-quart casserole.

Combine breadcrumbs and 2 tablespoons melted butter; sprinkle over casserole. Bake at 350° for 20 minutes or until hot and bubbly. Serve immediately. Yield: 8 servings.

oven, and garnish with chopped parsley. Spoon onto serving plates, and serve warm. Yield: 12 servings.

Sauce:

2 tablespoons butter or margarine
2 tablespoons all-purpose flour
1 cup milk
1 tablespoon Chablis or other dry white wine
¼ cup (1 ounce) shredded sharp Cheddar cheese
¼ teaspoon Worcestershire sauce
⅛ teaspoon hot sauce
¼ teaspoon salt
Dash of white pepper
Dash of red pepper

Melt butter in a heavy saucepan over low heat; add flour, stirring until smooth. Cook 1 minute, stirring constantly. Gradually add milk; cook over medium heat, stirring constantly, until mixture thickens. Stir in wine, cheese, Worcestershire sauce, hot sauce, salt, and pepper; continue cooking over medium heat just until cheese melts and mixture is well blended. Yield: about 1 cup.

Note: Casserole may be assembled 1 day in advance. Cover and refrigerate overnight. Let casserole come to room temperature before baking.

Stuffed Egg and Mushroom Casserole and Spinach Quiche.

STUFFED EGG AND MUSHROOM CASSEROLE

12 hard-cooked eggs
1 (4.5-ounce) jar whole mushrooms, drained and minced
2 tablespoons butter or margarine, melted
1 tablespoon Worcestershire sauce
¼ teaspoon hot sauce
¼ teaspoon salt
Dash of white pepper
Dash of red pepper
1 (4.5-ounce) jar whole mushrooms, drained
½ pound sliced bacon, cooked and crumbled
½ cup (2 ounces) shredded sharp Cheddar cheese
Sauce (recipe follows)
2 tablespoons chopped fresh parsley

Slice hard-cooked eggs in half lengthwise, and carefully remove yolks. Mash yolks in a medium mixing bowl; stir in minced mushrooms, melted butter, Worcestershire sauce, hot sauce, salt, and pepper, mixing until well blended.

Stuff whites with yolk mixture; press cut sides of stuffed eggs together, pressing gently to reassemble each egg. Place eggs in a lightly greased 10- x 6- x 2-inch baking dish. Arrange whole mushrooms over top. Sprinkle with half of bacon and cheese. Pour sauce over top of casserole. Sprinkle with remaining bacon.

Bake at 350° for 30 minutes or until bubbly. Remove from

There are twelve places symmetrically laid for this late 1800s breakfast (right); ten for expected guests, two for the unexpected. After melon, there are five other courses, explaining the odds and ends which will accompany the fish and meat courses. The syrup is in place for the final course. By 1890, the centerpiece of towering fruit so popular in the 1700s had given way to a less elaborate arrangement of flowers.

SPINACH QUICHE

Pastry for 9-inch deep-dish
  pie
¼ cup chopped green onion
2 tablespoons butter or
  margarine
1 (10-ounce) package frozen
  chopped spinach, thawed
  and drained
1 cup (4 ounces) shredded
  Swiss cheese
4 eggs, beaten
1 cup whipping cream
½ cup milk
½ teaspoon salt
½ teaspoon pepper
⅛ teaspoon ground nutmeg

Line a 9-inch quiche dish or
pieplate with pastry; trim excess
pastry around edges. Prick the
bottom and sides of pastry with
a fork. Bake at 400° for 3 minutes; remove from oven, and
gently prick with a fork. Bake an
additional 5 minutes. Cool on a
wire rack.

Sauté onion in butter in a
large skillet until tender. Remove from heat. Stir in spinach
and cheese.

Combine eggs, whipping
cream, milk, salt, pepper, and
nutmeg in a large mixing bowl.
Stir in spinach mixture; pour
into pastry shell.

Bake at 375° for 35 minutes
or until set. Let stand 10 minutes before serving. Cut into
wedges, and serve warm. Yield:
6 servings.

ARTICHOKE QUICHE

Pastry for 9-inch pie
1½ cups whipping cream
3 eggs, beaten
½ teaspoon salt
¼ teaspoon white
  pepper
Dash of red pepper
Dash of ground nutmeg
2 (6½-ounce) jars marinated
  artichoke hearts,
  undrained
6 green onions, finely
  chopped
1 cup (4 ounces) shredded
  Swiss cheese
1 tablespoon butter or
  margarine

Line a 9-inch quiche dish or
pieplate with pastry; trim excess
pastry around edges. Prick bottom and sides of pastry with a
fork. Bake at 400° for 3 minutes; remove from oven, and
gently prick with a fork. Bake an
additional 5 minutes. Let cool
on a wire rack.

Combine whipping cream,
eggs, salt, pepper, and nutmeg
in a medium mixing bowl; mix
well, and set aside.

Drain artichokes, reserving 2
tablespoons oil; set aside. Cut
artichokes into bite-size pieces;
set aside.

Sauté onion in reserved oil in
a small skillet until tender;
drain off oil. Stir in reserved artichoke pieces; spoon into prepared pastry. Pour whipping
cream mixture over onion and
artichokes; sprinkle cheese on
top, and dot with butter. Bake
at 375° for 45 minutes or until
set. Let stand 10 minutes before
cutting into wedges. Yield: 6
servings.

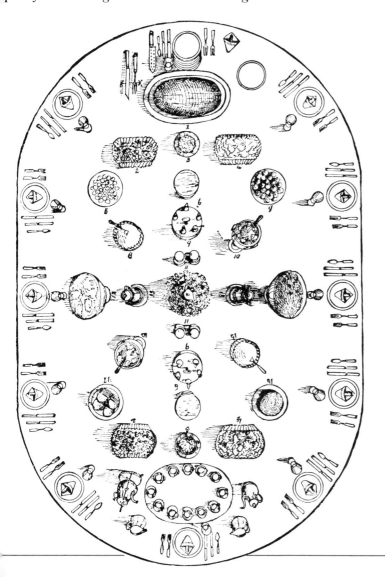

*The correctly set
breakfast table as
shown in* Practical
Housekeeping, *1890.*

1. Melon.	10. Butter.
2. Radish.	11. Pickles.
3. Spoons.	12. Dish Custard.
4. Lettuce.	13. Molasses
5. Fancy biscuit.	14. Oatmeal.
6. Dressing.	15. Loaf sugar.
7. Corn muffins.	16. Cake.
8. Powdered sugar.	17. Cold dry toast.
9. Caster.	18. White syrup.

Home demonstrators display cheese they made for the Federal "Live at Home" program. Virginia, 1939.

BACON-CHEESE CASSEROLE

¾ cup cornmeal
1½ cups water
2 cups (8 ounces) shredded
  Cheddar cheese
¼ cup butter or margarine,
  softened
1 teaspoon chopped fresh
  parsley
½ teaspoon salt
¼ teaspoon garlic powder
1 cup milk
4 eggs, separated
½ pound sliced bacon, cooked
  and crumbled

Combine cornmeal and water in a large heavy saucepan; cook over medium heat, stirring frequently, until mixture begins to thicken. Add cheese, butter, chopped parsley, salt, and garlic powder; stir until cheese and butter melt.

Combine milk and egg yolks, stirring well to blend. Gradually add milk mixture to cornmeal mixture, stirring constantly. Cook over medium heat, stirring constantly, until mixture thickens. Remove from heat, and fold in bacon.

Beat egg whites (at room temperature) until soft peaks form. Fold whites into cornmeal mixture, and pour into a well-greased 2-quart casserole. Bake at 325° for 1 hour or until a knife inserted in center comes out clean. Spoon onto serving plates, and serve immediately. Yield: 8 servings.

EASY CHEESE SOUFFLÉ

4 slices bread, crust removed
¾ cup milk
¼ cup butter or margarine
½ teaspoon salt
Pinch of red pepper
1 cup (4 ounces) shredded
  sharp Cheddar cheese
3 eggs, separated

Combine bread slices and milk in a medium saucepan. Cook over medium heat until bubbles appear around edge of pan. Stir in butter, salt, pepper, and cheese; cook mixture over low heat, stirring constantly, until butter and cheese melt.

Beat egg yolks in a medium mixing bowl until thick and lemon colored. Gradually stir one-fourth of hot cheese sauce into yolks; add to remaining cheese sauce, stirring constantly. Cook 1 to 2 minutes. Remove from heat. Let cool.

Beat egg whites (at room temperature) until stiff but not dry. Gently fold into cheese mixture. Spoon into a lightly greased 1-quart soufflé dish or casserole. Place in a pan of hot water; bake at 375° for 45 minutes or until browned and puffed. Serve immediately. Yield: 4 servings.

CHILE-CHEESE GRITS

1½ cups uncooked regular
  grits
3 eggs, beaten
1 pound Longhorn cheese,
  shredded
½ cup butter or margarine
1 (4-ounce) can chopped
  green chiles, undrained
1 tablespoon seasoning salt
Dash of hot sauce
Dash of paprika
Dash of Worcestershire sauce

Cook grits in a large saucepan according to package directions. Add eggs, cheese, butter, green chiles, seasoning salt, hot sauce, paprika, and Worcestershire sauce; stir well until cheese and butter begin to melt.

Pour grits mixture into a 13- x 9- x 2-inch baking dish; bake at 250° for 1½ hours or until set. Spoon onto serving plates, and serve warm. Yield: 12 servings.

CHEESY EGG CASSEROLE

4 cups (16 ounces) shredded
  Monterey Jack cheese
1 (4-ounce) can chopped
  green chiles, drained
4 (8-ounce) cartons
  small-curd cottage cheese
½ cup all-purpose flour
1 teaspoon baking powder
½ cup butter or margarine,
  melted
10 eggs, beaten

Combine cheese, green chiles, and cottage cheese in a large mixing bowl; stir well.

Sift together flour and baking powder. Add flour mixture, butter, and eggs to cheese mixture, mixing well.

Pour into a well-greased 13- x 9- x 2-inch baking dish. Bake at 400° for 15 minutes; reduce temperature to 350°, and cook an additional 30 minutes. Serve immediately. Yield: 10 servings.

Cheesy Egg Casserole makes a delicious, high-protein dish. Green chiles add an extra fillip.

CHEESE NEST EGGS

1 (2-pound) package process
  cheese spread, shredded
12 eggs
½ cup whipping cream
¼ cup dry mustard
Salt
Red pepper

Place cheese in a buttered 13- x 9- x 2-inch baking dish. Make 12 wells in cheese. Break one egg into each well.

Combine whipping cream and mustard in a small mixing bowl; stir well.

Spoon 2 teaspoons whipping cream mixture over each egg. Sprinkle with salt and pepper. Bake at 325° for 30 minutes or until eggs reach desired degree of doneness. Yield: 12 servings.

Note: This may be assembled and refrigerated a day ahead. Let come to room temperature before baking.

FOR HEARTIER TASTES

BROILED BRUNCH STEAKS

3 tablespoons butter or
   margarine, melted
2 tablespoons lemon juice
4 (¼-pound) cubed steaks
1 teaspoon salt, divided
½ teaspoon pepper, divided
4 slices bacon
4 (½-inch-thick) slices tomato
Fresh parsley sprigs

Combine butter and lemon juice; stir well, and set aside.

Sprinkle steaks with ½ teaspoon salt and ¼ teaspoon pepper. Place steaks on lightly greased rack in a shallow roasting pan; brush tops with half of lemon-butter mixture.

Broil steaks 6 inches from heating element 5 minutes; turn steaks, and brush with remaining lemon-butter mixture.

Place bacon on rack with steaks; broil an additional 3 minutes. Place one tomato slice on top of each steak; sprinkle with remaining salt and pepper. Crumble bacon; place equal amounts on top of tomatoes. Broil an additional 2 minutes.

Transfer steaks to a warm serving platter; garnish with parsley sprigs. Serve immediately. Yield: 4 servings.

COUNTRY-FRIED STEAK

4 (¼-pound) cubed steaks
1 teaspoon salt, divided
¼ teaspoon pepper, divided
1¼ cups milk, divided
1 cup plus 2 tablespoons
   all-purpose flour, divided
Vegetable oil

Sprinkle cubed steaks with ¾ teaspoon salt and ⅛ teaspoon pepper; dip in ¼ cup milk. Dredge steaks in 1 cup flour.

Heat oil in a large skillet over medium heat. Cook steaks 8 minutes or until golden brown, turning once. Remove steaks, reserving 2 tablespoons pan drippings in skillet. Drain steaks on paper towels, and keep warm.

Add remaining 2 tablespoons flour to pan drippings, stirring until smooth. Cook over low heat 1 minute, stirring constantly. Gradually add remaining milk; cook over medium heat, stirring constantly, until thickened and bubbly. Stir in remaining salt and pepper.

Transfer steak to a warm serving platter; serve immediately with gravy. Yield: 4 servings.

Beef on their plates and hats on their heads, cowboys enjoy breakfast at the Mulberry Ranch in the Texas Panhandle, c.1910

Panhandle-Plains Historical Museum

Corned Beef Hash with eggs nestled on the top has always been a favorite with men for a filling meal.

FRIZZLED BEEF

1 tablespoon butter or
  margarine
3 (⅛-inch-thick) slices cooked
  roast beef (about ½ pound)

Melt butter in a large skillet over medium-high heat. Add roast beef, and brown 1 minute on each side. Serve immediately. Yield: 4 to 6 servings.

CORNED BEEF HASH

3 cups finely chopped, cooked
  corned beef
3 cups peeled and coarsely
  chopped boiled potatoes
¼ cup whipping cream
⅓ cup chopped onion
3 tablespoons finely chopped
  fresh parsley
¼ teaspoon salt
Dash of pepper
2 tablespoons butter or
  margarine
6 eggs

Combine corned beef, potatoes, whipping cream, onion, parsley, salt, and pepper in a large mixing bowl; mix well.

Melt butter in a large skillet over low heat. Add corned beef mixture; press flat with a spatula. Cook, uncovered, over medium heat 15 minutes; stir once, and press flat again. Cook, uncovered, 15 minutes.

Make 6 indentions on top of hash mixture using back of a spoon. Add 1 egg to each indention. Cover skillet and cook an additional 5 minutes or until eggs reach desired degree of doneness. Serve immediately. Yield: 6 servings.

VEAL LOUISIANE

1 tablespoon lard
2 pounds veal round steaks,
  cut into 8 serving-size
  pieces
2 tablespoons all-purpose
  flour
2 cups water
2 medium-size green peppers,
  chopped
1 medium onion, chopped
2 tablespoons tomato paste
1 tablespoon chopped fresh
  parsley
½ teaspoon salt
¼ teaspoon pepper
¼ teaspoon red pepper
¼ teaspoon dried whole
  thyme
1 bay leaf
Hot cooked rice

Melt lard in a large skillet over medium heat. Add veal and cook 5 minutes or until brown, turning once. Remove veal from skillet, reserving pan drippings. Set veal aside.

Stir 2 tablespoons flour into pan drippings in skillet. Cook over medium heat, stirring constantly, 5 minutes or until flour is browned. Add remaining ingredients except hot cooked rice, mixing well. Cook mixture 1 to 2 minutes. Add reserved veal, and simmer, uncovered, 30 minutes or until veal is tender. Remove bay leaf, and discard. Serve veal with sauce over hot cooked rice. Yield: 8 servings.

Alice Moseley. Pope. Mississippi

Country Ham, Redeye Gravy, and Mama's Biscuits *by Mississippi artist Alice Moseley.*

PAN-FRIED PORK CUTLETS

1½ pounds pork tenderloin, cut into 6 serving-size pieces
1 teaspoon salt, divided
¼ teaspoon pepper, divided
½ cup all-purpose flour, divided
¼ cup vegetable oil
2 tablespoons bacon drippings
1½ cups milk
Fresh parsley sprigs (optional)

Flatten cutlets to ⅛-inch thickness using a meat mallet; sprinkle with ½ teaspoon salt and ⅛ teaspoon pepper. Dredge cutlets in ¼ cup flour.

Sauté cutlets in oil and bacon drippings in a large skillet over medium heat 2 minutes on each side or until lightly browned. Remove from skillet; set aside. Reserve drippings in skillet.

Add remaining ¼ cup flour to pan drippings, stirring until smooth. Cook over medium heat 1 minute, stirring constantly. Gradually add milk; cook, stirring constantly, until thickened. Add remaining salt and pepper.

Add cutlets to skillet, arranging over cream gravy. Cover and simmer 30 minutes, turning cutlets frequently. Remove cutlets to a serving platter; spoon gravy over cutlets, and garnish with parsley sprigs, if desired. Yield: 6 servings.

Note: Six (½-inch-thick) pork chops (about 1½ pounds) may be substituted for tenderloin; do not flatten.

SAUSAGE CAKES

1 egg, beaten
2 tablespoons water
1 pound bulk pork sausage
2 cups crushed corn flakes

Combine egg and water in a small mixing bowl; mix well.

Cut sausage into twelve patties. Dip each pattie in egg mixture, coating well; dredge in corn flake crumbs.

Cook patties in a large skillet over low heat, turning frequently, until browned and thoroughly cooked. Serve hot. Yield: 6 servings.

COUNTRY GRITS AND SAUSAGE

2 cups water
½ teaspoon salt
½ cup uncooked quick
   grits
4 cups (16 ounces) shredded
   sharp Cheddar cheese
4 eggs, beaten
1 cup milk
½ teaspoon dried whole
   thyme
⅛ teaspoon garlic powder
2 pounds mild bulk pork
   sausage, cooked, crumbled,
   and drained
Tomato roses
Fresh parsley sprigs

Bring water and salt to a boil; stir in grits. Return to a boil, and reduce heat. Cook 4 minutes, stirring occasionally.

Combine grits and cheese in a large mixing bowl; stir until cheese melts. Combine eggs, milk, thyme, and garlic powder, mixing well. Add a small amount of hot grits mixture to egg mixture, stirring well; stir into remaining grits mixture. Add crumbled sausage, stirring well. Pour mixture into a 12- x 8- x 2-inch baking dish. Cover and refrigerate overnight.

Remove from refrigerator; let stand 15 minutes. Bake at 350° for 50 to 55 minutes. Garnish with tomato roses and parsley sprigs. Yield: 8 servings.

Note: Recipe may be halved; bake at 350° in a 10- x 6- x 2-inch baking dish 45 minutes.

The Family Hominy Mill with Fan Attachment processed a bushel of corn an hour.

Maryland Historical Society

SAUSAGE-APPLE CORNBREAD

1 pound bulk pork sausage
6 peeled apple rings
1 cup all-purpose flour
1 cup yellow cornmeal
2 tablespoons sugar
1 tablespoon plus 1 teaspoon
   baking powder
½ teaspoon salt
1 cup milk
1 egg, beaten
Warm applesauce (optional)

Brown sausage in a large skillet over medium heat, stirring to crumble. Drain, reserving 2 tablespoons drippings. Set aside.

Arrange apple rings in bottom of a greased 9-inch pieplate; sprinkle one-third of sausage over apples. Set aside.

Combine flour, cornmeal, sugar, baking powder, and salt in a medium mixing bowl. Combine milk, egg, and reserved drippings; stir into dry ingredients, mixing well. Stir in remaining sausage. Pour cornbread mixture into prepared pieplate.

Bake at 425° for 30 minutes or until cornbread is golden brown. Remove from oven, and immediately invert pieplate onto a serving dish. Cut cornbread into wedges, and serve with warm applesauce, if desired. Yield: 6 servings.

SAUSAGE CASSEROLE

2 cups uncooked brown rice
1 pound hot bulk pork
   sausage
1 pound mild bulk pork
   sausage
2 cups chopped onion
2 cups chopped celery
2 (12-ounce) containers
   Standard oysters, drained
2 cups minced fresh parsley,
   divided

Prepare rice according to package directions; set aside.

Brown sausage in a Dutch oven, stirring to crumble. Add onion and celery; sauté until vegetables are tender. Drain off pan drippings.

Stir in reserved rice, oysters, and 1 cup parsley. Pour mixture into a 13- x 9- x 2-inch baking dish. Bake at 350° for 25 minutes. Remove from oven; sprinkle remaining 1 cup parsley over mixture, and bake an additional 5 minutes. Serve hot. Yield: 12 to 15 servings.

BAKED CANADIAN BACON

2 pounds Canadian bacon
½ cup beer
1 cup apple cider
1 cup firmly packed brown
   sugar
1 teaspoon prepared
   mustard
½ teaspoon ground cloves

Remove outer casing from bacon, if necessary. Place bacon in a lightly greased 9-inch square baking pan; pour beer over bacon. Bake, uncovered, at 350° for 15 minutes; baste once with pan juices.

Combine cider, sugar, mustard, and cloves in a medium mixing bowl; stir until sugar dissolves. Pour cider mixture over bacon; bake an additional hour, basting often.

Transfer bacon to a warm serving platter; slice and serve immediately with pan juices. Yield: 8 servings.

131

BACON GRILL

16 slices bacon
8 peach halves
6 cups cold, cooked mashed
  potatoes
2 eggs, beaten
1 teaspoon salt
¼ teaspoon paprika
½ cup all-purpose flour
¼ cup bacon drippings,
  melted and divided
Fresh parsley sprigs

Place bacon and peach halves on racks in 2 broiler pans.

Combine potatoes, eggs, salt, and paprika in a large mixing bowl; mix well. Shape mixture into 8 cakes; dredge in flour.

Place on racks with bacon and peach halves. Brush peaches and potato cakes with 2 tablespoons bacon drippings.

Broil 2 inches from heating element 6 minutes or until potato cakes are browned. Remove from oven, and turn peaches, bacon, and potato cakes. Brush peaches and potato cakes with remaining bacon drippings. Broil an additional 6 minutes or until browned.

Place potato cakes on a serving dish. Top each cake with 2 slices bacon and a peach half. Garnish with parsley. Serve immediately. Yield: 8 servings.

Ham Mousse and Asparagus with Chicken-Cheese Sauce.

HAM MOUSSE

1 envelope unflavored
  gelatin
¾ cup cold water
1 cup mayonnaise
2 cups chopped cooked ham
½ cup chopped celery
¼ cup chopped green pepper
1 teaspoon grated onion
½ cup whipping cream,
  whipped
Deviled eggs
Watercress sprigs
Fresh parsley sprigs

Combine gelatin and water in a saucepan. Cook over low heat until gelatin dissolves. Remove from heat. Add mayonnaise, beating well. Chill until consistency of unbeaten egg white.

Stir in next 4 ingredients. Fold in whipped cream. Pour into a lightly oiled 4-cup mold; chill until firm.

Unmold mousse onto a serving plate. Garnish with deviled eggs, watercress, and parsley. Yield: 8 to 10 servings.

ASPARAGUS WITH CHICKEN-CHEESE SAUCE

1 pound fresh asparagus,
  cleaned
2 tablespoons butter
2 tablespoons all-purpose
  flour
1 cup milk
1 cup (4 ounces) shredded
  sharp Cheddar cheese
¼ teaspoon grated lemon rind
2 cups chopped cooked
  chicken
½ teaspoon salt
¼ teaspoon white pepper

Cook asparagus; drain. Transfer to a serving platter; keep warm.

Melt butter in a saucepan; add flour, stirring until smooth. Gradually add milk; cook over medium heat, stirring constantly, until mixture is thickened. Add cheese; stir until cheese melts. Add lemon rind, chicken, salt, and pepper; mix well. Spoon sauce over asparagus. Yield: 4 servings.

Fresh produce and meat attracted customers to the Old Dutch Market, c.1918.

CHICKEN-BROCCOLI BAKE

1 (10-ounce) package frozen broccoli spears
4 chicken breast halves, cooked, skinned, and boned
2 tablespoons butter or margarine
2 tablespoons all-purpose flour
½ cup chicken broth
½ cup whipping cream
½ cup mayonnaise
Juice of ½ lemon
¼ teaspoon salt
⅛ teaspoon pepper
Dash of curry powder
½ cup (2 ounces) shredded sharp Cheddar cheese
1 cup crushed buttery round crackers

Cook broccoli according to package directions; drain well. Place chicken in a 10- x 6- x 2-inch baking dish; arrange broccoli over chicken. Set aside.

Melt butter in a heavy saucepan over low heat; add flour, stirring until smooth. Cook 1 minute, stirring constantly. Gradually add chicken broth and whipping cream; cook over medium heat, stirring constantly, until thickened and bubbly. Remove from heat. Stir in mayonnaise, lemon juice, salt, pepper, and curry powder. Pour sauce over broccoli. Sprinkle with cheese; cover with cracker crumbs.

Cover and bake at 350° for 30 minutes or until bubbly. Serve hot. Yield: 4 servings.

CREAMED CHICKEN

¾ cup butter or margarine
¾ cup all-purpose flour
6 cups milk
2 teaspoons salt
¼ teaspoon celery salt
6 cups diced, cooked chicken
6 hard-cooked eggs, finely chopped
Crunchy Corn Sticks (page 96)
Paprika

Melt butter in a small Dutch oven over low heat; add flour, stirring until smooth. Cook 1 minute, stirring constantly. Gradually add milk; cook over medium heat, stirring constantly, until thickened and bubbly. Stir in salt, celery salt, and chicken; continue to cook until thoroughly heated. Stir in chopped egg.

Spoon chicken mixture over Crunchy Corn Sticks; sprinkle with paprika. Serve immediately. Yield: 12 servings.

133

With stained glass and Tiffany fixture, this dining room is an elegant setting for a 1901 breakfast.

CHICKEN LOAF WITH ALMOND-MUSHROOM SAUCE

4 eggs, beaten
1 cup milk
½ cup chicken broth
2 teaspoons minced onion
1 teaspoon paprika
½ teaspoon salt
2½ cups diced, cooked chicken
¾ cup soft breadcrumbs
½ cup cooked regular rice
Almond-Mushroom Sauce
Fresh parsley sprigs

Combine eggs, milk, chicken broth, onion, paprika, and salt in a large mixing bowl; beat well. Stir in chicken, breadcrumbs, and rice. Pour mixture into a greased 8½- x 4½- x 3-inch loafpan. Place in a shallow pan containing 1 inch hot water.

Bake at 350° for 50 minutes or until a knife inserted in center comes out clean. Cool 10 minutes in pan; unmold onto a warm serving platter. Serve with Almond-Mushroom Sauce. Garnish with parsley. Yield: 6 to 8 servings.

Almond-Mushroom Sauce:

1 cup sliced fresh mushrooms
1 tablespoon minced onion
¼ cup butter or margarine
¼ cup all-purpose flour
2 cups chicken broth
2 teaspoons lemon juice
½ cup sliced almonds, toasted
Salt and pepper to taste

Sauté mushrooms and onion in butter in a medium skillet until onion is tender. Gradually add flour, stirring until smooth. Cook 1 minute, stirring constantly. Gradually add broth; cook over medium heat, stirring constantly, until thickened and bubbly. Stir in lemon juice, almonds, and salt and pepper. Serve hot. Yield: 2¼ cups.

SAUTÉED CHICKEN LIVERS

1 pound chicken livers, halved
¼ cup butter or margarine
¼ pound fresh mushrooms, sliced
1 small onion, sliced
1 teaspoon all-purpose flour
½ teaspoon salt
½ cup Chablis or other dry white wine
1 tablespoon finely chopped fresh parsley
½ teaspoon Worcestershire sauce
Toast points

Sauté livers in butter in a large skillet 5 to 6 minutes. Remove livers; add mushrooms and onion to pan drippings. Sauté until onion is tender. Stir in flour and salt. Add wine, parsley, and Worcestershire sauce; bring to a boil. Reduce heat, and simmer 3 to 5 minutes. Add livers; cook 5 minutes over medium heat. Spoon liver mixture over toast points. Serve warm. Yield: 4 servings.

CREAMED SALMON AND MUSHROOMS

1 (3-ounce) can sliced mushrooms, undrained
2 tablespoons butter or margarine
¼ cup all-purpose flour
1 cup whipping cream
1 (15½-ounce) can salmon, drained and flaked
6 baked commercial patty shells
Fresh watercress

Drain mushrooms; reserve liquid, and set aside.

Melt 2 tablespoons butter in a heavy saucepan over low heat; add flour, stirring until smooth. Cook 1 minute, stirring constantly. Gradually add whipping cream and reserved mushroom liquid; cook over medium heat, stirring constantly, until mixture is thickened and bubbly. Stir in salmon and mushrooms. Continue to cook until thoroughly heated.

Spoon creamed mixture evenly into patty shells. Garnish each with watercress; serve immediately. Yield: 6 servings.

Note: Cooked chicken, tuna, or any fish combination may be substituted for salmon.

HOT SEAFOOD SALAD

2 cups cooked, peeled medium shrimp
1¼ cups lump crabmeat
2 cups diced celery
1 medium onion, chopped
4 hard-cooked eggs, diced
1 (8-ounce) can sliced water chestnuts, drained
1 (4-ounce) can mushroom pieces and stems, drained
½ teaspoon salt
1½ cups mayonnaise
½ cup slivered almonds
½ cup soft breadcrumbs

Combine first 8 ingredients in a large bowl; stir well. Fold in mayonnaise; blend well. Spoon into a lightly greased 2½-quart casserole. Sprinkle with almonds and breadcrumbs.

Cover and bake at 350° for 30 minutes. Spoon onto serving plates, and serve hot. Yield: 6 to 8 servings.

SHRIMP WITH HOMINY

½ cup butter or margarine
1 pound medium shrimp, peeled and deveined
½ teaspoon salt
¼ teaspoon pepper
1 (16-ounce) can hominy, undrained
Paprika
Fresh parsley sprigs

Melt butter in a small saucepan over medium heat. Add shrimp, salt, and pepper; sauté until shrimp are thoroughly heated. Cover and cook an additional 5 minutes. Remove from heat, and keep warm.

Place hominy in a small saucepan; cook over medium heat until thoroughly heated. Drain and transfer hominy to a serving bowl. Spoon shrimp over hominy; drizzle butter left in skillet over shrimp, if desired. Sprinkle with paprika; garnish with parsley. Serve hot. Yield: 4 servings.

Shrimp with Hominy is a favorite combination.

BREAKFAST SHRIMP

2 tablespoons chopped onion
2 teaspoons chopped green pepper
3 tablespoons bacon drippings
1½ cups small shrimp, peeled and deveined
1 cup plus 3 tablespoons water, divided
2 tablespoons all-purpose flour
1 tablespoon catsup
1 teaspoon Worcestershire sauce
½ teaspoon salt
¼ teaspoon pepper
Hominy

Sauté onion and green pepper in bacon drippings until tender. Stir in shrimp; sauté 2 to 3 minutes. Add 1 cup water, and simmer an additional 2 to 3 minutes, stirring occasionally.

Combine flour and remaining water; mix well, and stir into shrimp mixture. Add catsup, Worcestershire sauce, salt, and pepper; stir well. Continue to cook over low heat until sauce thickens, stirring frequently.

Remove shrimp mixture to a warm serving bowl. Serve immediately with hominy. Yield: 4 servings.

Grits label, 1930, features state capitol at Baton Rouge.

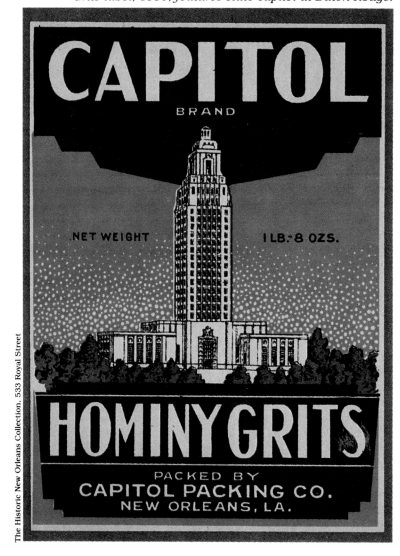

BROILED TROUT

2 tablespoons butter, melted
4 freshwater trout fillets (about 1 pound)
1 tablespoon lemon juice
½ teaspoon seasoning salt
¼ teaspoon dried whole basil
Lemon wedges (optional)

Line a shallow baking pan with aluminum foil. Brush foil with melted butter. Place fish on foil; sprinkle with lemon juice, salt, and basil.

Broil fish 6 inches from heating element 5 minutes or until fish flakes easily when tested with a fork. Transfer fish to a warm serving platter. Garnish with lemon wedges, if desired, and serve immediately. Yield: 2 to 4 servings.

BROILED SALT MACKEREL

1½ pounds salt mackerel fillets
3 cups milk
Juice of 1 lemon
3 tablespoons butter or margarine, softened
¼ teaspoon pepper
Chopped fresh parsley

Place fish in a large shallow container; pour milk over fish. Cover and refrigerate overnight.

Drain fish. Place fish in a small Dutch oven with water to cover; bring to a boil. Boil 5 minutes or until fish is tender.

Place fish on rack in a shallow roasting pan. Rub with lemon juice and butter; sprinkle with pepper. Broil fish 6 inches from heating element 5 minutes or until fish flakes easily when tested with a fork.

Transfer fish to a warm serving platter, and sprinkle with parsley. Serve immediately. Yield: 4 servings.

Elaborate trade card for corn cereals, c.1883.

cACKNOWLEDGMENTS

Almond Puff Coffee Cake, Artichoke Quiche, Cheese Nest Eggs, Cheesy Egg Casserole, English Muffins, Icebox Potato Rolls, Mississippi Spice Muffins, Petite Blueberry Muffins, Stuffed Egg and Mushroom Casserole, Turkey Hash adapted from *Southern Sideboards* by the Junior League of Jackson, ©1978. By permission of The Junior League of Jackson, Mississippi.

Alsatian Pancakes adapted from *Our Favorite Recipes*. Published in 1982 by Castro Colonies Heritage Association, Castroville, Texas.

Apple Roll adapted from *Generation to Generation*, compiled by Barbara Dybala and Helen Macik, ©1980. By permission of the Historical Society of the Czech Club, Dallas, Texas.

Apricot Nut Bread adapted from *Nashville Seasons Cook Book* by The Junior League of Nashville, ©1964. By permission of the Junior League of Nashville, Inc., Tennessee.

Asparagus with Chicken-Cheese Sauce, Chicken-Broccoli Bake adapted from *A Taste of Tampa* by the Junior League of Tampa, ©1981. By permission of The Junior League of Tampa, Florida.

Baked Stuffed Tomatoes adapted from *Talk About Good!* by the Junior League of Lafayette, ©1969. By permission of The Junior League of Lafayette, Louisiana.

Beignets, Café au Lait adapted from *La Bonne Cuisine*. Published in 1980 by La Bonne Cuisine, River Ridge, Louisiana.

Blueberry Muffins, Cream Cheese Wafers adapted from *Georgia Heritage - Treasured Recipes*. Published in 1979 by The National Society of The Colonial Dames of America in the State of Georgia.

Blueberry Pancakes adapted from *Plantation Recipes* by Lessie Bowers, ©1959. By permission of Robert Speller and Sons, Publishers, Inc., New York.

Braided Coffee Cake, Easy Cheese Soufflé, menu for Mooreland Hunt Breakfast, Sour Cream Omelet adapted from *Huntsville Heritage Cookbook* by The Grace Club Auxiliary, ©1967. By permission of The Grace Club Auxiliary, Huntsville, Alabama.

Burritos de Huevos con Chorizo courtesy of Mrs. JoAnn R. Macias, El Paso, Texas.

Chicken Loaf with Almond-Mushroom Sauce adapted from *The Nashville Cookbook* by Nashville Area Home Economics Association, ©1977. By permission of Nashville Area Home Economics Association.

Chile-Cheese Grits, menu for Mexican Breakfast adapted from *Seasoned with Sun* by the Junior League of El Paso, Texas, ©1974. By permission of the Junior League of El Paso, Inc., Texas.

Chocolate Fluff adapted from *Three Hundred Ways to Serve Eggs*, edited by Ruth Berolzheimer. Published in 1950 by Consolidated Book Publishers, Chicago, Illinois.

Cinnamon Rolls, Swedish Tea Ring adapted from *Martha White Southern Baking Book*, ©1983. By permission of Martha White Foods, Inc., Nashville, Tennessee.

Claret Lemonade adapted from *The Gasparilla Cookbook* by The Junior League of Tampa, ©1961. By permission of The Junior League of Tampa, Florida.

Cornmeal Muffins, menu for Thanksgiving Breakfast adapted from *Maryland's Way* by Mrs. Lewis R. Andrews and Mrs. J. Reaney Kelly. By permission of The Hammond-Harwood House Association, Annapolis, Maryland.

Cornmeal Patty Cakes adapted from *Gay Nineties Cook Book*, compiled, written, edited by F. Meredith Dietz and August Dietz, Jr., ©1945. By permission of The Dietz Press, Inc., Richmond, Virginia.

Cottage Cheese Pancakes, Mother Thomas' Corn Light Bread adapted from *The James K. Polk Cookbook* by The James K. Polk Memorial Auxiliary, ©1978. By permission of The James K. Polk Memorial Auxiliary, Columbia, Tennessee.

Dining car, page 23, owned by The Heart of Dixie Railroad Club, Birmingham, Alabama.

Everlasting Bread adapted from *Southern Cooking* by Mrs. S.R. Dull, ©1941, by S.R. Dull. By permission of Grosset and Dunlap, New York.

Fredericksburg Orange Doughnuts, Pineapple Fritters adapted from *Fredericksburg Home Kitchen Cookbook*, published by The Fredericksburg Home Kitchen Cookbook Central Committee, 1957.

Fresh Fig Muffins, Potato Griddle Cakes adapted from *The Treasure Chest of Old Southern Recipes*, published by the millers of LaFrance Flour, Dallas, Texas.

Gingerbread Waffles, Sweet Potato Waffles adapted from *The Gardener's Cookbook*, edited by Mildred W. Schlumpf.

Ham Mousse adapted from *Party Potpourri* by The Junior League of Memphis, ©1971. By permission of Memphis Junior League Publications, Memphis, Tennessee.

Hot Caramel Fruit courtesy of Mrs. Cheryl Landreth, Pleasant Grove, Alabama.

Menu for Brunch at Magnolia Hall courtesy of the Natchez Garden Club, Natchez, Mississippi.

Menu for Second Breakfast at Mme. Bégué's based on recipes adapted from *Mme. Bégué's Recipes of Old New Orleans Creole Cookery*.

Mulled Cider adapted from *Savannah Sampler Cookbook* by Margaret Wayt DeBolt, ©1978. By permission of The Donning/Company Publishers, Norfolk, Virginia.

Painting on page 30 copyright © Mattie Lou O'Kelley. By permission of Little, Brown and Company.

Pear Honey adapted from *Harvest Heritage* by The Junior Service League of Bay City, Texas.

Robert Morris Inn Cranberry Muffins courtesy of the Robert Morris Inn, Oxfood, Maryland.

Rumbled Eggs adapted from *Dr. Price's Cream Baking Powder Recipes*, published in 1905.

Rum-Butter Coffee Cake adapted from *Recipes and Party Plans, A Cookbook for the Hostess* by Sadie LeSeuer.

Sausage-Apple Cornbread courtesy of *Owens Country Cookbook* by Owens Country Sausage, Owens Spring Creek Farm, Richardson, Texas.

Scrambled Eggs and Rice courtesy of LaVerne Seidenstricker, Tollville, Arkansas.

Shad Roe with Bacon adapted from the *Maryland Seafood Cookbook III* by The Maryland Department of Economic and Community Development, Annapolis, Maryland.

Soda Biscuits courtesy of Joanne Thomas, Philadelphia, Mississippi.

Strawberry labels, page 12, courtesy of The Historic New Orleans Collection, 533 Royal Street, New Orleans, Louisiana.

Text on page 15 adapted from *The Aristocratic Journey*, published in 1931.

Weidmann's Eggs Benedict courtesy of Weidmann's Restaurant, Meridian, Mississippi.

Collection of Bonnie Slotnick

INDEX